11 95

An Introduction
to the
EPISCOPAL CHURCH

J.B. BERNARDIN

MOREHOUSE PUBLISHING

Copyright © 1935, 1940, 1957, 1978, 1983

Morehouse Publishing
P.O. Box 1321
Harrisburg, PA 17105

Fifth Edition (Updated)
13th Printing, 2001
ISBN 0-8192-1231-8

Printed in the United States of America

Preface

Multitudes of subconsciously-remembered ideas from friends and speakers and books go into the making and phrasing of any writing intended to cover a vast subject for popular use. To all of them an author would, if he were able, give grateful thanks for the help which they have been to him in his thinking. But only their ideas and not their names remain. He can, however, acknowledge the gracious kindness of those who read the first manuscript in 1935 and enabled him, by their suggestions, to avoid some of the pitfalls inevitably attendant upon generalization, and to indicate matters which he had neglected to treat. The Rev. Drs. Frederic M. Adams, Edward R. Hardy, Otis R. Rice, Howard C. Robbins, George A. Trowbridge, and Williams L. Savage, Esq. did this friendly service, and I am grateful for their generously-given help.

Forty years on, only two of these friends are alive today. As the Church and the world have continued increasingly to grow and change throughout this period, the necessity has arisen for a complete revision of the text. The Rev. Dr. Cotesworth P. Lewis and Mr. Timothy J. Kenslea of the Editorial Department of Morehouse Publishing have read the present manuscript and made challenging criticisms which have been eminently helpful. To them, as well as to the many down the years who in person or by letter have made suggestions about the book, I am deeply grateful.

J.B. BERNARDIN

All Saints' Day, A.D. 1977,
Williamsburg, Virginia.

CONTENTS

Chapter I

The Church's History

In the course of history there have been many and various forms of religion, some of which no longer exist and a large part of which never obtained more than local or temporary importance. Today there are eleven living world religions, among which is Christianity. Much of its teaching and isolated beliefs may be found in these other religions, but in one thing it is unique—it alone among all the revealed religions claims that God Himself made the revelation of Himself in the Person of His Son Jesus Christ, and thereby showed us what God was like and what God wanted us to be like; and that He imparts to us today the strength necessary to fulfil this purpose, if we seek it according to His will. The other religions claim that the divine revelation came through a prophet, as in Islam, or else through some lesser god, as in the ancient Hermetic cults, but never through the Supreme God Himself.

Jesus Christ, in order to perpetuate the revelation which God had made in Him, gathered about Himself a group of disciples from whom He chose an inner circle

which were known as the Twelve, and later as the
Apostles. At the time of His death on the cross they all
deserted Him, but after His resurrection He inspired them
with new hope and they went forth to carry to the world
the Gospel, the good news about the salvation to be obtained through faith in Him.

For the first hundred years or so of Christian history
the early disciples expected the imminent return of Christ
from heaven in glory to judge the world. Consequently,
they made no provision for the future or the carrying on
of their message beyond their own generation. The early
development of the Church came as a result of its adjust-
ment to the fact of the delayed return of Christ.

The first Jerusalem disciples continued to worship in
the Temple, forming a synagogue of the Nazarene, which
differed from the other synagogues only in their belief
that Jesus Christ was the Messiah predicted by the Scriptures, and that He was about to return to judge the world
and to inaugurate His Kingdom. After the persecution and
death of St. Stephen, the first Christian martyr, the
cleavage between Judaism and the followers of Jesus
Christ became apparent, and they were scattered to other
cities. Small groups of Christians became organized in
various places into assemblies or churches, meeting in
private houses. They were sometimes founded by the informal methods of traders, friends, or neighbors;
sometimes by the direct preaching of traveling disciples.

The earliest churches were ruled by the apostles
themselves. But as they were not always present, a share
in the government fell to the older men in the assembly,
just as it did in the Jewish synagogues. The word for elder
in Greek is one which has been anglicized as "presbyter,"
and in course of time shortened to priest. From this council of older men sprang the second order of the Christian

ministry, the priesthood. As time went on the need of someone to take the place of the apostles and to oversee the other elders was felt, and one among their number was chosen for this office of overseer. From the Greek word meaning overseer came *episcopus* in Latin, which in the course of time became anglicized as "bishop." The early Christians were mostly from the lower orders of society and of small means, and they not only suffered financially in many cases for their new beliefs, but also took little thought for the future on account of their expectation that the end of the world was near. Hence the problem of relief of the poor was a pressing one. The apostles felt that they could not take the time from their preaching necessary to attend to such work, so a body of officials was appointed to take charge of this and to visit the sick. They were called by a word in Greek which means "servant" and from which we get the English "deacon." They were the origin of the first order of the Christian ministry.

St. Paul was the one chiefly instrumental in the process by which Christianity grew from a purely Jewish and Asiatic religion to be a Gentile and European one as well. Quietly but doggedly Christianity grew and spread throughout the Roman Empire in spite of the fact that it was an illegal religion, despised by the ruling classes, and often persecuted by the State.

The last and severest persecution of Christianity under the Emperor Diocletian was followed by the Edict of Toleration issued by the Emperor Constantine in 311. From that time on increasing privileges were granted to Christianity until finally it became the official religion of the Empire. Church buildings began to be erected and the Church grew rapidly in numbers and wealth under Constantine. In 325 at Nicaea he assembled the first general council of the whole Church to pass on disputed points of doctrine and discipline, and from then on general councils have been held at intervals. In the year 1054 the Church in the East and the Church in the West, which had been increasingly estranged from one another since the ninth century, formally separated and have remained so ever since.

Long before this time Christianity has come to Britain. Unauthenticated tradition attributes it to St. Joseph of Arimathaea who is supposed to have come to Glastonbury with the Holy Grail. In all probability it was due to converted Gallic merchants and Roman soldiers. St. Alban, the first Christian martyr in Britain, suffered death there in the third century, and about the year A.D. 300 bishoprics are known to have existed at London, York, and Lincoln. But when the Roman legions were withdrawn in 401, the Christians were soon driven by the invading barbarians to the west of England and Wales, and even over into Ireland. In the next century the attempt to reconvert England was begun by two distinct missions. One came over from Ireland to Iona under St. Columba and worked down from the north; the other was the famous mission sent by Pope Gregory the Great under St. Augustine, which established itself at Canterbury in the year 597, and worked up from the south. As a consequence of this the Archbishop of Canterbury became the leading bishop of the Church of England. It took another century and the devoted labors of numerous saints before England was once again, at least nominally, Christian.

The English bishops in the course of time came more and more under the authority of the Pope, as did the English king John, who became his feudal fief. But as the popes began to abuse their authority and to exact heavy financial payments, a revolt gradually began to set in after the Black Death in 1349 with the passing of the Statutes of Provisors and *Praemunire* forbidding appointments to English bishoprics or benefices, or appeals to courts outside the realm, without the king's consent.

Throughout the Dark Ages the Church not only maintained the culture and learning of the ancient civilized world, but also looked after the social needs of the people through its own religious communities, caring for the poor, the sick, and the wayfarers. With the dawn of the Renaissance, and influenced in no small degree by the continental reformation of the Church initiated by Luther, inflamed by disgust at the moral corruption of the papacy and clergy, and brought to a head by an unworthy personal controversy of Henry VIII with the Pope over the question of annulment, parliament more and more restricted papal authority in England until, in 1534, it was declared that the Bishop of Rome had no authority over the bishops of the Church of England. In spite of the momentous consequences of this decision, the ordinary Christian was little affected at first by this decree, for he continued to worship in his same parish church and cathedral in the Latin tongue and to receive the sacraments from the hands of the same ministers as formerly. Henry VIII died no less orthodox and catholic than when the Pope conferred on him the title, still claimed by English sovereigns, "Defender of the Faith." Before the final breach with Rome, Henry had obtained the appointment of Thomas Cranmer as Archbishop of Canterbury, and Cranmer took a leading part in the reformation of the Church of England.

When Henry VIII died in 1547 he was succeeded by his nine-year-old son Edward VI, who was controlled in turn by his uncle, the Duke of Somerset, as Protector, and then by the Duke of Northumberland. Under them, in response to strong urging on the part of the people who wished further to purify the Church of England of what they considered unscriptural elements and unholy practices, the service books were first translated into English, and drastic reforms were made in the conduct and practice of worship.

Edward VI was succeeded in 1553 by his half-sister Mary, who restored the papal authority and the Latin service, and put to death some of the bishops who refused to take the oath of obedience of the Pope, including Archbishop Cranmer of Canterbury. In 1558 she was succeeded by her half-sister, Elizabeth, who once more repudiated the authority of the Pope over the Church of England and issued a revised English Prayer Book in 1559. In 1570 Elizabeth was excommunicated by the Pope. This marks the formal withdrawal of the Church of Rome from communion with the Church of England. Although England repudiated the authority of the Bishop of Rome, she did not withdraw from fellowship with the Church of Rome, but Rome from her. But centuries before this the Church of England, mentioned in the *Magna Carta* of 1215, had been established by law as the official Church of the realm of England, and it was authorized to receive land taxes, known as tithes, for its support.

During Elizabeth's reign the new country to the west was being opened up and explored. It was a chaplain of the flagship of Sir Francis Drake who, on the shores of Golden Gate Bay in San Francisco in the year 1579, held the first Prayer Book service in this country. Various parts of America were settled by different religious groups. Florida and Maryland were founded by the Roman Catholics; New England by the Puritans or Congregationalists; Rhode Island by the Baptists; New York by the Dutch Reformed; Pennsylvania and New Jersey by the

Friends; Delaware by the Swedish Lutherans; and Virginia, North Carolina, South Carolina and Georgia by the Church of England.

The first permanent English settlement was made at Jamestown, Virginia in 1607, where the Rev. Robert Hunt preached and administered the sacraments. The direct successor of that congregation still exists today as Bruton Parish, Williamsburg, Virginia. From there the Church of England spread into Maryland, and in these two states it became established by law as in England, and received tithes for its support.

In spite of much opposition the worship of the Church began to be held in Boston at King's Chapel in 1687. With the coming of the English governor to New York in 1664 Church of England services were held, after those in Dutch, in the old Church of St. Nicholas within the Fort. Trinity Parish was organized in 1697 and a year later moved into its own church building. In Philadelphia Christ Church was founded as early as 1695.

By the time of the Revolutionary War there were congregations of the Church of England in all of the colonies, chiefly, however, in the larger towns along the seaboard. Many of these were assisted greatly by two missionary societies, then recently formed in England by the Rev. Dr. Thomas Bray, which still exist today: the Society for Promoting Christian Knowledge, founded in 1699 and commonly known by its initials as the S.P.C.K., and the Society for the Propagation of the Gospel in Foreign Parts, founded in 1701 and now known as the U.S.P.G.

Throughout all these years not only was no bishop appointed for the colonies, in spite of many petitions on their part, but none ever visited them. Nominally they were under the jurisdiction of the Bishop of London. In consequence, Confirmation was never administered, and anyone wishing to be ordained had to make the perilous voyage back to England, which greatly hindered the development of a native ministry.

When the Revolutionary War broke out, though there were priests like Dr. William White of Christ Church, Philadelphia, who became Chaplain not only of the Continental Army but also of the Continental Congress, the majority of the clergy remained loyal to the King. Consequently, after the war was over, the Church suffered in prestige, in spite of the fact that the majority of the signers both of the Declaration of Independence and of the Constitution of the United States were its members.

In the year 1783 the Church in Connecticut elected the Rev. Dr. Samuel Seabury as its bishop and sent him to England to be consecrated at the hands of the English bishops. This they refused to do because he could not take the oath of allegiance to the King, and they had no authority without parliamentary sanction to dispense with it. Tiring of the delay, he turned to the Scottish nonjuror bishops, who had remained loyal to the House of Stuart and were consequently not recognized by the State nor bound by the laws of the Established Church, and was consecrated by them at Aberdeen, Scotland, on November 14, 1784. In the years 1784-86 conventions of the various Churches were held to decide what course of action should be taken. In 1787 Dr. Samuel Provoost, Rector of Trinity Church, New York, and Dr. William White, Rector of Christ Church, Philadelphia, went to England and were consecrated bishops in Lambeth Palace Chapel by the Archbishops of Canterbury and York, the Bishop of Bath and Wells, and the Bishop of Peterborough, a law having been enacted to make this possible; and later, in 1790, Dr. James Madison was also consecrated in England as Bishop of Virginia. In the year 1789 at Philadelphia a General Convention was held at which a Constitution was adopted for the Church and the English Prayer Book revised for American needs.

The Episcopal Church grew slowly in numbers, for in the eighteenth century the prevalence of Deism (rationalistic, naturalistic religion) was widespread, and most of the clergy were indifferent to missionary endeavor. As the tide of emigration swept westward beyond the Alleghenies they refused to follow, and the vast field of the Central States and the Middle West was left to the Methodists and the Baptists to evangelize. Finally, however, influenced by the Great Awakening under John and Charles Wesley and George Whitefield, came a revival of personal religion and evangelistic endeavor, and the Episcopal Church awoke to its missionary responsibility, largely due to the efforts of Bishop John Henry Hobart in New York and Bishop Alexander V. Griswold in New England. Bishop Philander Chase was consecrated Bishop of Ohio in 1819. The following year the Domestic and Foreign Missionary Society was incorporated, and in 1835 General Convention declared that every member of the Episcopal Church by virtue of his membership was also a member of the Missionary Society. In this same year Bishop Jackson Kemper was consecrated Bishop of the Northwest; and by the time of the Gold Rush the Episcopal Church was fully alive to its responsibility and Bishop William I. Kip was sent to California.

The General Theological Seminary for the education of men for the ministry of the Episcopal Church was opened in New York City in 1819; and shortly afterwards the Theological Seminary in Virginia was established at Alexandria with special emphasis on preparing men for missionary work. Since then many more have been founded throughout this country and also overseas.

The nineteenth century saw the flowering of the Evangelical Movement with its emphasis on personal piety and good works; then in polarity to it, the Anglo-Catholic or Oxford Movement, with its emphasis on the catholicity and apostolicity of the Church, and a revival of interest in church ceremonial, ritual, and catholic practice. At the same time the Church was faced with the problems produced by the new scientific knowledge in conflict with biblical and creedal statements, particularly in Charles Darwin's theory of evolution; and also by the growth of biblical criticism, in which the books of the Bible were investigated and studied by the same methods of literary and historical criticism as any other writing.

The Episcopal Church weathered the Civil War without any permanent division into North and South such as was the fate of most of the larger denominations at that time. In the second half of the century sisterhoods and monastic orders for men were established in the Episcopal Church, as well as secondary, industrial, and mission schools, several colleges, and numerous hospitals. Mission fields were developed in the various territorial possessions and dependencies of the United States; and the Episcopal Church, by the end of the nineteenth century, had taken its rightful place in the forefront of the religious life of the country. With the increasing interest in the beauty of worship, church buildings and cathedrals expressive of the highest in art and architecture were built, and music of appropriate dignity and beauty maintained.

In the interest of the efficient management and further development of so vast an organization, the central administration of the Episcopal Church was reorganized in 1919 under a National Council which carries on the functions of General Convention between its triennial meetings. Two years earlier the Episcopal Church, in order to provide adequate retirement allowances for its clergy and pensions for their direct dependents in case of death, established its Pension Fund, which has become a model for those of other denominations.

In 1872 the Woman's Auxiliary to the Board of Missions was organized, which in 1920 broadened the scope of its work to include other activities of the Church besides missions in its program, and became the Woman's Auxiliary to the National Council. In 1889 it started the United Thank Offering (a voluntary, monetary expression of gratitude for God's blessings on the part of the women, placed in a little blue box), which has become one of the chief supports of the Church's missionary and educational work. In recent years the Woman's Auxiliary has become the Episcopal Churchwomen; and the National Council has been renamed the Executive Council.

In 1934 the Forward Movement was inaugurated to stimulate the spiritual life of the Church. It proposed a disciple's rule of life: Turn—Follow—Learn—Pray—Serve—Worship—Share. It continues to publish helpful devotional booklets. At the Anglican Congress in 1963, in order to bring about a rebirth of the Anglican Communion, the concept of Mutual Responsibility and Interdependence in the Body of Christ (MRI) was set forth. Numerous dioceses have linked themselves in mutual aid and support with a companion diocese within the Anglican Communion.

The Episcopal Church, as well as the whole Anglican Communion, has been one of the leaders in the ecumenical movement for the restoration of the visible unity of the Church. Bishop Charles H. Brent in 1910 initiated steps which resulted in the formation of the World Council of the Churches in 1948 at Amsterdam, with all of the leading Churches of the Anglican Communion as members. In addition, the Episcopal Church is also a member of the National Council of the Churches of Christ in the United States of America, which was constituted in 1950 out of thirteen interdenominational agencies. It is also one of the original members of the Consultation on Church Union (COCU), seeking the organic union of many of the larger American Protestant Churches.

The twentieth century has also been marked by an increased participation of the laity in the work, worship, and governance of the Church. Persons other than white (they now number 52% of the Anglican Communion) have taken a more prominent and equal place in the Church's life, and women a more active part in its governance — in 1976 they were authorized to be ordained to all three orders of the ministry. The early part of the century found much emphasis on the Social Gospel, particularly in its application to the relations between capital and labor. More recently there has been an emphasis on Liberation Theology, dealing with the problems of the poor and the oppressed, particularly in the less developed countries. At the same time there has been an increased interest in worship and its study, spurred by the Liturgical Movement begun in the previous century. It has resulted in the production of revised and elaborated forms of worship, not only in the Anglican Communion, but in the Roman Catholic and Protestant Churches as well.

In reviewing the Church's history, it is important to remember that it is as new as it is old; that it was founded by our Lord Himself, and in the course of its history has seen many forms of government and used many languages in its worship; but that, while outwardly the Church adapts itself efficiently to the circumstances of the time, within there is enshrined the tradition which is received from the apostles of the revelation of God in the Person of Jesus Christ, as illuminated for every age by the Holy Spirit.

BOOKS FOR FURTHER READING

BARCLAY, W., *Jesus of Nazareth*. New York: Ballantine, 1989.

_____, *The Mind of Jesus*. San Francisco: HarperSF, 1976.

BEVAN, E. R., *Christianity*, reprint. Westport, CT: Greenwood Press, 1981.

Book of Saints, A Dictionary of Servants of God. Compiled by the Benedictine monks of St. Augustine's Abbey, Ramsgate. Harrisburg, PA: Morehouse Publishing, 1993.

CROSS, F. L. and LIVINGSTONE, E. A., eds., *The Oxford Dictionary of the Christian Church*, 2nd ed. New York: Oxford University Press, 1958, 1974, 1983.

FARMER, D. H., *The Oxford Dictionary of Saints*. Oxford: Oxford University Press, 1987, 1992.

LATOURETTE, K. S., *A History of Christianity*. San Francisco: HarperSF, 1953.

MOORMAN, J. R. H., *A History of the Church in England*. Harrisburg, PA: Morehouse Publishing, 1972.

NEILL, S., *Anglicanism*, 4th ed. Oxford: Oxford University Press, 1977.

PRICHARD, R. W., *A History of the Episcopal Church*. Harrisburg, PA: Morehouse Publishing, 1991.

_____, *Readings from the History of the Episcopal Church*. Harrisburg, PA: Morehouse Publishing, 1986.

SUMNER, D. E., *The Episcopal Church's History 1945-1985*. Harrisburg, PA: Morehouse Publishing, 1987.

Chapter II

The Church's Government

The Church which our Lord founded has four notes or characteristics, which are summed up in the creedal phrase the "One, Holy, Catholic, and Apostolic Church." The first of these is *unity*. Our Lord founded only one Church and meant His followers to be one in Him. He is not responsible for the various sects into which Christianity is now divided. The second note is *holiness*. Holy originally meant to be set apart for the Diety, to be sacred. The Church was intended to be set apart from evil unto righteousness. Its members were to live lives distinguished from those without the Church by their likeness to the life of their Lord. The Church and its members belong to God. The third is *catholicity* or universality. Our Lord intended His Church to be for people of every kindred and clime, of every degree of wealth, social position, and education. It was not to be a local Jewish Palestinian club, but an organization to embrace the whole of the human family. The fourth of these is *apostolicity*. The Church was to be founded with the inner circle of his followers, the Apostles, as its first members and leaders, and it was they who were to proclaim His message to all people after His death.

In the course of time the Church has unfortunately been divided into a large number of communions, which can be divided roughly into two group, popularly called "Catholic" and "Protestant." The Catholic groups includes the Church of Rome, the Old Catholics, the Greek Orthodox Church, and various national Churches in the East. The Protestant group includes, first of all, the Lutheran Church which owes its origin to Martin Luther; and various Reformed Churches which owe their origin to John Calvin, among which are the Huguenots, the Dutch Reformed, and the Presbyterian Churches. In later times the Baptist, Congregational, Methodist and other Protestant Churches arose. However, the Church of England, of which the Protestant Episcopal Church in the United States is the daughter, is both Catholic and Protestant.

The essential features of a Catholic Church are, first, that it should have a three-fold ministry of bishops, priests, and deacons ordained by bishops who stand in line of succession from the apostles, generally called the apostolic succession or historic episcopate; secondly, that it should have the Catholic creeds, the so-called Apostles' and Nicene; thirdly, that it should have the Bible; and fourthly, that is should have the sacraments ordained by our Lord, Baptism and the Holy Communion. These are the essential bases for the union of the Episcopal Church with any other Church, as outlined in the Chicago-Lambeth Quadrilateral of 1886—1888.

The chief characteristics of a Protestant Church are, first of all, that from which the name comes—its protest, or witness to, or setting forth of the fundamental truths of the Gospel, and its protest against the unique authority of the Pope or Bishop of Rome over other bishops and clergy, his right to rule all Christians, and to arrogate to himself the power which has become his in the course of time; secondly, the use of the vernacular tongue in its worship; thirdly, the simplicity of its ceremonial; and fourthly, the freedom of the conscience of individual Christians in the matter of religious practice, although this last has been more an ideal than a fact.

As can be seen, the Episcopal Church fulfills the conditions of both and has consequently been called the "Bridge Church." Its general position has been that of a *via media* or golden mean between two extremes. It is a Church which strives to maintain in essentials unity; in non-essentials liberty; and in all things charity. The legal title is a cumbrous but significant one: THE PROTESTANT EPISCOPAL CHURCH IN THE UNITED STATES OF AMERICA. It is a Protestant Church in that it both bears witness to the Gospel of God and protests against the Pope's claim to authority over other bishops. It is Episcopal in that it is governed by bishops; and it is confined (with a few exceptions) to the United States of America and its present or former possessions.

An Episcopal Church is governed by bishops; a Presbyterian Church by presbyters or elders; and a Congregational Church by the congregation. The Episcopal Church, although governed by bishops, is also democratically ruled, for its final authority rests in the General Convention, which meets every three years. It consists of a House of Bishops and a House of Deputies. Each diocese of the Church is entitled to send four clerical and four lay delegates. Similarly, each diocese is governed by a diocesan convention which meets annually, and to which every parish is entitled to send a certain number of lay delegates, in addition to its clergy.

As the Constitution of the Episcopal Church was drawn up in 1789 by many of the same men who helped to write the Constitution of the United States, there are many parallels between the two forms of government. General Convention is similar to the Congress; consisting of two houses, the House of Bishops corresponding to the Senate, and the House of Deputies to the House of Representatives. The Presiding Bishop corresponds to the President of the United States, and the Executive Council to the Cabinet. The dioceses correspond to the states, the diocesan conventions to the state legislatures, and the bishops to the governors. The administrative divisions of dioceses are like counties. Parishes are like cities, vestries like town councils, and rectors like mayors. All the members of the Church share directly or indirectly in its government through their election of representatives. In parishes the communicants elect the vestries, and usually, the delegates to diocesan conventions. The latter elect delegates to the General Convention.

The Church is divided, first of all, into parishes presided over by rectors. They may have one or more ordained assistants (sometimes called curates), and also lay assistants, such as parish visitors, directors of religious education and organists. Sometimes within a parish there may be dependent congregations known as chapels or missions and presided over by vicars. Parishes are grouped together into dioceses presided over by bishops; dioceses into provinces presided over by archbishops; these in turn are joined together into patriarchates presided over by patriarchs. In the Episcopal Church there are no archbishops at the head of provinces and no patriarchates; but instead there is an elected administrative head of the Church, known as the Presiding Bishop, who is also President of the Executive Council, a body formed to supervise and stimulate the work of the Church. It also acts as the Board of Directors of the Domestic and Foreign Missionary Society, whose constitution dates back to 1821. It is the legal body which holds the endowment funds of the Church.

A large professional staff is maintained at the Church's headquarters (815 Second Avenue, New York, New York 10017) to assist the clergy and laity in carrying on the work of Christ in the five fields of service: the parish, the community, the diocese, the nation, and the world. In addition there is a bishop specially charged with the Church's work with the American armed forces at home and abroad.

Some dioceses are subdivided into archdeaconries for missionary purposes, and these are in charge of archdeacons. Others are divided, or further subdivided, into rural deaneries or convocations in charge of a rural dean. In the Church a dean is the head of a cathedral, the principal church in a diocese located in the see city, in which the bishop has his throne or seat. The title "dean" is also given to the heads of theological seminaries.

Parochial clergy, whether deacons or priests, are addressed in writing as "The Reverend John Doe"; archdeacons as "The Venerable John Doe"; deans of cathedrals as "The Very Reverend John Doe"; bishops as "The Right Reverend John Doe"; and archbishops as "The Most Reverend John Doe." In conversation, male parochial clergy are called Mr. Doe, Father Doe, or Dr. Doe, and female Miss Doe, Mrs. Doe, or Dr. Doe, depending on their preference and whether or not they possess a doctor's degree from some institution of learning. Archdeacons, deans, bishops, and archbishops are usually referred to in this country by those titles and their own names, as "Dean Doe," but in other countries by the title of their office, as "the Dean of X." Lay members of male religious communities are addressed as "Brother John" and ordained members as "Father Doe." Members of female religious communities are addressed as "Sister Jane" and their heads generally as "Mother Jane."

The Preamble to the Church's Constitution begins: "The Protestant Episcopal Church in the United States of America, otherwise known as The Episcopal Church (which name is hereby recognized as also designating the Church), is a constituent member of the Anglican Communion, a Fellowship within the One, Holy, Catholic, and Apostolic Church, of those duly constituted Dioceses, Provinces, and regional Churches in communion with the See of Canterbury, upholding and propagating the historic Faith and Order as set forth in the Book of Common Prayer".

The Episcopal Church is an independent part of this larger whole, which includes: the Church of England (2 provinces), the Church in Wales, the Church of Ireland (2 provinces), the Episcopal Church in Scotland, the Protestant Episcopal Church in the United States of America (9 provinces), the Anglican Church of Canada (4 provinces), the Anglican Church of Australia (5 provinces), the Church of the Province of New Zealand, the Church of the Province of Southern Africa, Nigeria Tegarideria the Church in the Province of the West Indies, Nippon Seikokai (Japan), Chung Hua Sheng Kung Hui (China), the Church of the Province of West Africa, the Church of the Province of Central Africa, the Episcopal Church in Jerusalem and the Middle East, the Church of Burundi, Rwanda, and Zaire, Igreja Episcopal do Brasil, the Church of the Province of Burma, the Church of the Province in Tanzania, the Church of the Province of Kenya, the

Province of the Episcopal Church of the Sudan, the Church of the Province of Melanesia, the Church in the Province of The Indian Ocean, the Church of the Province of Papua New Guinea, the Church of the Province of West Africa, the Iglesia Anglicana Del Cono Sud de Las Americas, and a number of extra-provincial dioceses scattered throughout the world. Approximately every ten years the bishops of these Churches consult together at the Lambeth Conference in England.

In addition, there is a body of Churches known as the Wider Episcopal Fellowship possessing the historic episcopate, with which the Episcopal Church is in either full communion or a relationship of intercommunion. Among these are the Old Catholic Churches, the Philippine Independent Church, united churches containing former Anglican dioceses, such as those of South India, Pakistan, and North India, Bangladesh and a number of other national Churches.

BOOKS FOR FURTHER READING

Constitution and Canons for the Government of the Protestant Episcopal Church in the United States of America, (revised every three years).

The Episcopal Church Annual. Harrisburg, PA: Morehouse Publishing, (revised annually).

HOLMES, U. T. III, *What is Anglicanism?* Harrisburg, PA: Morehouse Publishing, 1982.

MCADOO, H. R., *The Unity of Anglicanism: Catholic and Reformed.* Harrisburg, PA: Morehouse Publishing, 1983.

Chapter III

The Church's Bible

All religions of civilized peoples possess collections of sacred writings which they regard as an authoritative revelation of the nature of their deity and of his will. In every case these writings were written by religiously-minded men to meet the needs and situation of their own day. Tradition soon endowed them with a divine origin and a sacrosanct authority. Consequently, in later times it became necessary either to revise them or make interpolations in the text; or else to resort to an allegorical exegesis in order to fit them to the religious needs of succeeding generations. What is true of the sacred books of other religions, is also true of the Bible, the sacred book of Christianity.

The Bible means books. It is a collection of writings ranging in date from about the year 900 B.C. to A.D. 150, written by men of religious insight for the needs of their own generation, and in many cases revised by others in succeeding years for their own times. The Bible is divided into two parts: the Old Testament, comprising 39 books, and the New Testament, containing 27; although a better translation of the Greek titles would be the Old Covenant and the New Covenant.

The Old Testament contains a record of God's relation to humanity and humanity's relation to God under the covenant which He made with them under Abraham, and which was renewed under Moses at Mount Sinai: namely, that if they would be circumcised and keep His covenant He would be their God and give to them the land of Canaan for an everlasting possession. Similarly, the New Testament contains the record of God's relation to humanity and humanity's relation to God under the covenant which He made with them in Jesus Christ; namely, that those who believe in Him and are baptized into His Name and keep His commandments will obtain everlasting salvation.

The Old Testament was originally written in Hebrew, except for a few short passages in Aramaic. In the Hebrew Bible it is divided into three parts: the Law, comprising the first five books of the Bible, supposed to have been written by Moses; the Prophets, divided into the Former Prophets (our historical books) and the Latter Prophets, comprising the three major prophets, Isaiah, Jeremiah, and Ezekiel, and the twelve minor prophets; and the Writings. The earliest and the most sacred of these was the Law which in its present form dates from the time of Ezra about 444 B.C. The prophetical canon, that is, the books forming the Prophets, was formed about 250 B.C., but the final decision as to just what books comprised the Writings was not made until a council held in Jamnia in Palestine toward the end of the first century A.D.

In the course of time Hebrew became a dead language, and it was necessary to translate these writings into other languages in order that the people might understand them. The two principal translations were that into

Aramaic for the people of Palestine, called the Targum, and that into Greek for those outside, called the Septuagint. The Greek Old Testament contains in addition to the books found in the Hebrew Bible a number of others.It was this Greek Old Testament which was the sacred book of the early Christian Church and out of which they claimed to prove the birth, death, and resurrection of our Lord.

At the time of the Continental Reformation Luther and the other reformers rejected the books of the Old Testament which were found only in Greek, and not in Hebrew, and which still form part of the Bible of the Church of Rome and the Eastern Churches. The English Church, as often, took a middle position. Removing these books from their usual order, it placed them together in a group between the Old and the New Testament and labelled them the Apocrypha, declaring that they were to be read for example of life and instruction of manners, but not for the establishment of any doctrine. Parts of them are among the most beautiful and helpful passages in the whole Bible and will repay a careful reading.

The earliest Christian writings, so far as we know, were *testimonia,* or collections of Old Testament texts supposedly predicting the events in our Lord's life, which were used in controversy with the Jews. Next come collections of our Lord's sayings. Both of these, as well as the forms into which oral preaching had become stereotyped, were made use of later when men began to draw up accounts of the good news that salvation had come to the world through Jesus Christ—the writings which we call Gospels. The earliest of these is the Gospel according to St. Mark, written by him in Greek about the year 65 in Rome for the use of the Church there and, according to an early tradition, based on the reminiscences of St. Peter. St. Mark aims chiefly to give an outline of the major events of our Lord's ministry; to prove that He was the Son of God, and to show why, nevertheless, it was necessary for Him to be put to death; and to encourage Christians by His example to endure the sufferings to which they were subjected.

Another Gospel was written for a Church in a predominantly Jewish neighborhood, possibly Antioch, about the year 80, based chiefly on the Gospel according to St. Mark and a lost collection of sayings of our Lord which scholars call Q (from the German *Quelle,* "source"), with some additional material of its own. This is known as the Gospel according to St. Matthew, and was written to prove that Jesus was the promised Messiah as foretold by Scripture.

St. Luke, the Gentile companion of St. Paul, wrote a Gospel about the year 85 for some Gentile Church, based on St. Mark and Q, with additional material of his own. His work shows particular interest in the Holy Spirit, in prayer, in the poor, in women, and in works of mercy. About the year 100 another Gospel was written, possibly for the Church in Ephesus, called the Gospel according to St. John, which was composed around seven great miracles, or signs, to show that Jesus was the Christ, the heavenly Son of God, and that those who thus believe might have life through His Name. Although the most spiritual in its interpretation of the Person and meaning of Christ, it is not the most historical as to the actual events of His life, and the speeches there attributed to Christ are almost invariably the composition of the unknown author himself. These four Gospels were the first to be accepted by Christians as inspired sacred writings equal in authority to the Hebrew Scriptures, and they form the first part of our New Testament.

The next part is an account of the activities of two of the chief followers of our Lord, St. Peter and St. Paul, showing how Christianity spread from Jerusalem to Rome, or in other words, how it became a universal as opposed to a local religion. It was written by St. Luke about the year 95 as a continuation of the Gospel composed by him and is called the Acts of the Apostles.

Long before the Gospels were written, however, apostles, absent from their Churches, sent them letters of encouragement and advice which were treasured in their archives and copies of which were sent to other Churches. The earliest and best known collection of these is the Epistles of St. Paul, which form the next section of the New Testament, although some of the fourteen letters included therein are now known not to be his work. Most of them were written to meet some particular need in the local Church, and are not to be taken as complete statements of either Christian doctrine or practice at that time, or as St. Paul's entire views on the subjects mentioned. The two Epistles addressed to St. Timothy and the one to St. Titus are commonly known as the Pastoral Epistles, and are in all probability the work of a Pauline disciple. The Epistle to the Hebrews is the work of an unknown teacher, worried about the erroneous doctrines his pupils were absorbing in his absence, who sent them this letter to confirm them in the Faith.

The next group of writings is the seven Catholic Epistles, so-called because supposed to be addressed to the Church as a whole, although this is only partly true. The last book of the New Testament is the Revelation of St. John the Divine, modeled on similar Jewish apocalypses. It was written during the persecution under Domitian, about 96, to encourage Christians to remain true to the Faith and to refuse to join in the worship of the Roman Emperor, by showing them under well-known symbols the blessed reward of the saints and martyrs in heaven and the destruction and future punishment of Rome.

Although the above outline of dates is fairly conventional, it should be pointed out that there are scholars who hold other dates, and even some who believe that all of the New Testament was written before the fall of Jerusalem in A.D. 70.

The latest book of the New Testament to be composed, the so-called Second Epistle of St. Peter, was written about 150, but it was not until the second half of the fourth century that the canon of the New Testament, that is, the list of writings which were to be esteemed sacred and inspired alongside of the ancient Jewish Scriptures, was finally decided upon as we now have it. The Church was in existence, then, for some three hundred years before it finally made a definite decision as to just what books were to comprise its Bible. Long before this time a large part of its members could no longer understand Greek. Consequently, translations were made in the third century into languages which they could comprehend: Syriac for the Eastern Churches, Coptic for the Egyptian, and Latin for the Western. This last was the common Bible in the West, particularly in the translation made by St. Jerome and known as the Vulgate, down to the time of the Reformation in the sixteenth century, when various translations into the common vernacular tongues were made. Of these Luther's translation into German is the most famous.

In England there was a translation of the Gospels into Anglo-Saxon as early as the year 1000; and of the Bible into Middle English in the time of John Wyclif about 1380. Since the Reformation there have been several

English translations of varying merit; among them Tyndale's New Testament (1525), Coverdale's Bible (1535), and the Great Bible (1539), from which the Psalter in the original Prayer Book was taken.

The historic Bible of the Episcopal Church is that known as the Authorized Version, or King James Version, because the translation was published in 1611 at his instigation. The Revised Version of this appeared in 1881, the American Standard Version in 1901, and the Revised Standard Version in 1952. The last is an accurate, dignified translation into modern American English based on the results of the latest biblical scholarship. In 1973 an ecumenical edition of this appeared known as the Common Bible. There are also four completely new idiomatic translations into contemporary English: the Roman Catholic Jerusalem Bible (1966) and New American Bible (1970), the New English Bible (1970), and the Good News Bible (the Bible in Today's English Version, 1976). All of these are authorized for use in the services of the Episcopal Church. Possibly the New English Bible is the most helpful for personal reading.

A knowledge of the Bible is essential to any correct understanding of Christianity, and the only way in which it can be acquired and maintained is by some systematic scheme of reading it. There are various books issued containing plans for daily Bible reading, and there is also the table of the daily lessons appointed to be read in Church, which can be found at the end of the Prayer Book.

Not only is the Bible the source-book for a knowledge of Christianity and one of the great literary heritages of all ages, both in its original languages and in its English Authorized Version; it is also the world's greatest book in its power to comfort and sustain people in their trials, to inspire them to that which is good and beautiful, to guide them in their perplexities, to lift their thoughts heavenward, and to bring them into closer fellowship with the God of all good life.

BOOKS FOR FURTHER READING

BARCLAY, W., *Daily Study Bible: New Testament*, 18 vols., rev. ed. Philadelphia: Westminster/John Knox, 1975.

_____, *Great Themes of the New Testament*. Philadelphia: Westminster/John Knox, 1979.

BENNETT, R. A. and EDWARDS, O. C., *The Bible for Today's Church*. San Francisco: HarperSF, 1979.

BORSCH, F. H., *Anglicanism and the Bible*. Harrisburg, PA: Morehouse Publishing, 1984.

BUTTRICK, G. A., ed., *The Interpreter's Bible*, 12 vols. Nashville, TN: Abingdon Press, 1952-57.

CULLMANN, O., *The New Testament: An Introduction for the General Reader*. Philadelphia: Westminster/John Knox, 1968.

HUNTER, A. M., *Introducing the New Testament*, 3rd ed. Philadelphia: Westminster/John Knox, 1972.

LEWIS, C. S., *Reflections on the Psalms*. New York: Harbrace, 1985.

METZGER, B. M., *An Introduction to the Apocrypha*. New York: Oxford University Press, 1957.

PARMALEE, A., *Guide to the Old Testament and Apocrypha*. Harrisburg, PA: Morehouse Publishing, 1979.

_____, *Guide to the New Testament*. Harrisburg, PA: Morehouse Publishing, 1979.

SANDMEL, S., ed., *The New Oxford Annotated Bible with the Apocrypha*. New York: Oxford University Press, 1977.

SPRAGUE, M. S., *One to Watch, One to Pray: A Devotional Introduction to the Gospels.* Harrisburg, PA: Morehouse Publishing, 1988.

Chapter IV

The Church's Prayer Book

Worship is a witness to the worth of somebody or something. Hence Christian worship is a testimonial to the supreme worth of the one God of the universe, as He has manifested Himself as Father, Son, and Holy Spirit. It is accompanied by praise and thanksgiving and the offering of a sacrifice — the oblation of oneself, the giving back to God of the free will with which He has endowed us.

The earliest worship of the Christians followed the order used in the Jewish synagogue: Psalms; the reading of the Scriptures; the comment on the Scriptures, or sermon; and prayers. In the course of time the Psalms, Scriptures, and prayers were arranged in seven offices to be said at seven different periods throughout each day (although in practice they were often combined), and collected in a book known as the Breviary.

In addition, the early Christians met in the evening for a common meal of fellowship, known as an Agape or Love Feast. At the end of it they broke the bread and blessed the wine in thankful remembrance of the benefits

33

which they had received from Christ's death, believing that in partaking of this Bread and Wine they were doing what their Lord had commanded them to do and were sharing in His Life. As time went on this celebration was divorced from the Agape and placed in the morning. The prayers which accompanied it became standardized in different localities, generally reflecting the usage of the principal Church of that region, and were contained in books known in the West as Missals.

The Church of England until the Reformation had its various service books in Latin, but in the reign of Edward VI in the year 1549 these were simplified, translated into English, and combined into one book called the Book of Common Prayer. The liturgical practice at the Cathedral at Salisbury, known as the Sarum Rite, was the one chiefly followed. Three years later a revised book was issued which was little used. During the reign of Queen Mary the Church of England reverted to the Latin Service Books, but in 1559 in the reign of Elizabeth the Prayer Book of 1552, slightly revised, was reissued in English. It underwent a minor revision in 1604 under James I and a more extensive one under Charles II in 1662. This is still the official Prayer Book of the Church of England and was the one used in the American colonies.

After the Revolutionary War at the General Convention of the American Church in Philadelphia in 1789 (the year of President Washington's inauguration), the first American Prayer Book was published, being a revision of the English Prayer Book of 1662, but in nowise departing from it in any essential of doctrine, discipline, or worship. This Prayer Book went through several slight revisions in succeeding years. In 1892 a more complete revision was made, and again in 1928. This revision not only brought the prayers more into conformity with modern thought, but also the service itself into closer agreement with the best liturgical usage, and made provision for greater freedom in the arrangement of the daily services. To the measured and restrained Elizabethan English of the 1928 and earlier Prayer Books is due in no small measure the beauty of Anglican worship as it has existed throughout four centuries.

After more than ten years of study and trial use, a radically new Book of Common Prayer was adopted in 1979. In it the Daily Offices, Collects, Eucharist, and Burial Service are found in traditional language, as well as in the contemporary, in which the rest of the Book is composed. When there are two Rites, the following explanations apply only to Rite I.

Any change or alteration in the Prayer Book (except in the tables of Psalms and Lessons) must be passed by two succeeding General Conventions before it becomes effective. The present form of worship has gone through many stages and changes in the long history behind it. The Prayer Book contains prayers and blessings as old as the sixth century B.C. and as modern as the twentieth century A.D.

The Prayer Book opens with prefatory matter in regard to the conduct of worship, the feasts and fasts to be observed, and the Calendar of the Church year. Following this comes the first section of the Prayer Book, containing the Daily Office, derived chiefly from the ancient breviaries. Morning and Evening Prayer are intended to be said daily, and the structure of the two services is the same, although there are some differences. They are printed in both a Traditional (I) and a Contemporary (II) form.

They begin with an invitation to worship (the opening sentences), and may be followed by a general confession of sins, and a general absolution. The confession comes here in order that the hindrance of sin may be removed and the soul set free of any barrier between itself and God. The confession is really one of sinfulness rather than of sins, and in one's private prayers before and at that time it should be made an individual confession of particular sins.

Then comes a section of praise, beginning with a versicle (a short verse mostly from the Psalms) and response, the *Gloria Patri*, and an invitatory (consisting of an antiphon), followed by the *Venite* (a cento of the 95th and 96th Psalms), or the *Jubilate* (the 100th Psalm), and followed by the recitation of part of the Psalter. Then follow one or two lessons, each followed by a canticle chosen from among the *Benedicite, Benedictus es, Magnificat, Nunc Dimittis, Gloria in excelsis, Te Deum,* or others. The Apostles' Creed is then said standing, the people customarily facing the cross on the altar. After this come the prayers, beginning with the salutation, the Lord's Prayer (which is found in every service in the Prayer Book, and is always to be said by the people along with the minister), the suffrages (versicles and responses), the collect of the day, other collects and prayers, and the grace (from the ending of St. Paul's Second Epistle to the Corinthians).

Evening Prayer follows the same outline with some variation as to content. Then follows Rite II of Morning Prayer, composed in contemporary language and using the same order as Rite I, but including more canticles. It also uses, both here and elsewhere, the translations proposed by the International Consultation on English Texts (ICET) for the Lord's Prayer, Creeds, and Canticles, with some slight changes. Then come contemporary orders of service for Noonday, for Candle-lighting, Evening Prayer Rite II, and Compline (the last monastic service of the day, traditionally said at 9 p.m.). This section concludes with Daily Devotions for Individuals and Families.

The Great Litany in traditional language comprises the next section. A litany is a liturgical prayer consisting of a series of invocations, deprecations (for deliverance from evil), obsecrations (entreaties for help), suffrages, *Agnus Dei, Kyrie,* and the Lord's Prayer, followed by the Supplication. The minister often kneels at a litany desk below the chancel to lead it.

The next section consists of the Collects for the Church Year, first in their traditional, and then in their contemporary form. It is arranged in three parts: the Sundays from Advent I (including the Holy Days between Christmas and the Epiphany) through Trinity Sunday; the Sundays for the Season after Pentecost, to be used according to their nearness to fixed calendar dates; and Holy Days arranged in calendrical order. In addition there are collects for special occasions.

Proper Liturgies for Special Days is the next section, which includes special services for Ash Wednesday, Palm Sunday, Maundy Thursday, Good Friday, and the Easter Vigil.

Holy Baptism, the next section, is intended to be administered within the Eucharist, but may be performed separately. It follows the eucharistic order through the sermon. Then follow the presentation of the candidates and their renunciations, the baptism covenant and promises, prayers, the blessing of the water, the baptism, the sealing, and the peace. The service may continue with

Confirmation, Reception, or Reaffirmation, and the Eucharist, or else may end with the Lord's and other prayers.

The Holy Eucharist, The Liturgy for the Proclamation of the Word of God and Celebration of the Holy Communion, forms the next section. Eucharist is a Greek word meaning "thanksgiving" and is given to the prayer of consecration as well as to the whole rite, because it is a thanksgiving to God for the life and death of Jesus Christ, and the great benefits which we receive thereby.

The service originated in the words and actions of our Lord at the Last Supper. By the second century an assembly was held on Sunday where the memoirs of the apostles or the prophets were read by a reader, and then the president gave an exhortation, after which they all arose and offered prayers. Then bread and wine and water were brought and the president offered up prayers and thanksgivings and the people said *Amen.* After this came the distribution, the deacons taking it to those not able to attend. Then there was a freewill offering. Gradually fixed orders of service began to be developed, and we find the Liturgy of St. James in use at Jerusalem, the Liturgy of St. Mark at Alexandria, and the Liturgies of St. Basil and St. Chrysostom at Constantinople. In addition the Syrian, Coptic, and other Churches had in their own languages orders of service peculiar to themselves.

In the Latin West there were two distinct usages: the Roman and Gallican. The earliest extensive example of the Roman is that of the Leonine Sacramentary of the sixth century, followed by the Gelasian of the seventh, and later the eighth-century Gregorian Sacramentary. The English usage developed from that of Rome as found in the Sarum Rite. The American Liturgy is derived from the

English, but follows the Scottish usage in its prayer of consecration.

This eucharistic section first contains an Exhortation, then an optional Penitential Order: Rite I, and then the Holy Eucharist: Rite I, which opens with a versicle and response, all standing, followed by the Collect for Purity, that the people's hearts may be cleansed worthily to worship God, followed by an optional recitation of the Summary of the Law, followed by the *Kyrie* or *Trisagion* and *Gloria in excelsis.*

Next come the salutation and the Collect of the Day. A collect is a short prayer according to a standard form, consisting of an address, statement about the person addressed, petition, desired result of petition, and conclusion, in which one particular idea is collected or summed up. Then comes an Old Testament Lesson or the Epistle or both. These are customarily read from the epistle corner of the altar (the right as one faces it), or else from an ambo (a reading desk or pulpit), while the people sit. Between the lessons and the Gospel, a psalm, hymn, or anthem, known as the Gradual, may be sung. Then, all standing, the Gospel is read from the gospel corner of the altar (the left as one faces it), or from an ambo or the pulpit or after a procession to the center of the church. This is immediately followed by the Sermon, which traditionally is an explanation of the Gospel read. On Sundays and major feasts the congregation then declares its faith in the Gospel by the recitation of the Nicene Creed. Then follow the Prayers of the People, after which comes the Confession of Sin, if the Penitential Rite has not been used, and then the Peace. (The personal greeting of one another is optional). At this point ends the first half of the service, known as the *Synaxis*, or Mass of the Catechumens, or the Word of God.

The second half, designated The Holy Communion, begins with the offering of the bread and wine and the alms brought by the people to the altar, all standing. There follows the *Sursum Corda,* Proper Preface, *Sanctus,* and *Benedictus qui venit.* At this point most people kneel, and the celebrant says the prayer of consecration, divided into four parts: the narrative of the institution; the oblation (offering) of what is consecrated unto God, including a memorial (anamnesis) of Christ's death, resurrection, and ascension; the invocation *Epiclesis* of the Word and Holy Spirit; the conclusion. The bread and wine have been consecrated by the whole prayer to be the Body and Blood of Christ—it is impossible, according to liturgiologists, to pinpoint the exact moment of consecration—and are offered to the Father, along with the offerings of one's self to him, praying at the same time for the forgiveness of one's sins and for a mutual indwelling of Christ and oneself. The congregation then acknowledges our Lord's Presence in the Sacrament by repeating the prayer which He taught, after which comes the Fraction, where the priest breaks the consecrated bread, followed by silence. Then may come the *Pascha nostrum,* the *Agnus Dei,* and the Prayer of Humble Access (which the people may join in saying). The priest and the congregation then partake of the Sacrament, and thereby enter into spiritual communion and fellowship with God and with one another, and nourish their souls on the self-sacrifice of His love; after which thanks are returned to Him for this communion, and the blessing is given, followed by an optional dismissal.

There follow an alternative Prayer of Consecration, Offertory Sentences, and Proper Prefaces. Then comes a Penitential Order: Rite II in contemporary language, the Holy Eucharist: Rite II with three alternate prayers of consecration and six different Prayers of the People. An order is provided for the administration of the Reserved Sacrament, as well as an order for an informal Eucharist.

Pastoral Offices is the title of the next section, containing the Confirmation Service, a Form of Commitment to Christian Service, the Celebration and Blessing of a Marriage, a Thanksgiving for the Birth or Adoption of a Child, the Reconciliation of a Penitent, Ministration to the Sick (including scripture readings, laying on of hands and anointing with oil, Holy Communion, and prayers) and Ministration at the Time of Death. There follows the Burial of the Dead in both a traditional and a contemporary form. This service follows the outline of the eucharistic service, although if the Eucharist is not to be celebrated, the service may end with the Commendation. There is also an outline for a burial service where the regular one is not appropriate.

Episcopal Services, based on the old Pontifical, come next and consist of separate services for the ordination of bishops, priests, and deacons, a Litany for Ordinations, the Celebration of a new Ministry (in the case of a rector his Institution) and the Dedication and Consecration of a Church.

The next section contains the Psalter, the ancient hymn book of the Jews, composed at various times in their history. David was traditionally regarded as the author, but very few, if any, of the Psalms are from his hand or time. The 150 Psalms are divided into units to be read at Morning and Evening Prayer during the thirty days of the month. If there are thirty-one days, those for the thirtieth are generally repeated.

Following this comes a section of Prayers and Thanksgivings, some in traditional and some in contemporary language. The next section is An Outline of the

Faith, commonly called the Catechism. This is a modern, helpful statement of the principal Christian Beliefs. There follows a section called Historical Documents of the Church, containing the Chalcedonian Definition, the Athanasian Creed, the Preface to the 1549 Book of Common Prayer, the Thirty-nine Articles of Religion, and the Chicago-Lambeth Quadrilateral. There follow a section on Tables for Finding Holy Days; and then a section on the Lectionary, which contains three cycles of Psalms and readings for the Sundays, and one cycle for Holy Days and Various Occasions. Cycle A begins with Advent Sunday of years evenly divisible by three. The last section contains the Daily Office Lectionary in two cycles. Cycle A begins on Advent Sunday preceding odd-numbered years. This concludes the Book of Common Prayer.

BOOKS FOR FURTHER READING

ATKINSON, C. W., *A Lay Minister's Guide to the Book of Common Prayer.* Harrisburg, PA: Morehouse Publishing, 1988.

DAVIES, J. G., ed., *The New Westminster Dictionary of Liturgy and Worship.* Philadelphia: Westminster/John Knox, 1986.

HATCHETT, M. J., *Commentary on the American Prayer Book.* San Francisco: HarperSF, 1985.

HOWARD, T., *The Liturgy Explained.* Harrisburg, PA: Morehouse Publishing, 1981.

The Hymnal 1982 Companion, 3 vols., R. Glover, ed. New York: The Church Hymnal Corp., 1982-94.

JONES, C., WAINWRIGHT, G., and YARNOLD, E., eds., *The Study of Liturgy.* New York: Oxford University Press, 1978.

MICHNO, D. G., *A Priest's Handbook: The Ceremonies of the Church,* 2nd ed. Harrisburg, PA: Morehouse Publishing, 1986.

MITCHELL, L., *The Meaning of Ritual.* Harrisburg, PA: Morehouse Publishing, 1977.

_____, *Praying Shapes Believing, A Theological Commentary on The Book of Common Prayer.* Harrisburg, PA: Morehouse Publishing, 1985.

PRICE, C. P. and WEIL, L., *Liturgy for Living.* San Francisco: HarperSF, 1984.

STEVENSON, K. and SPINKS, B., eds., *The Identity of Anglican Worship.* Harrisburg, PA: Morehouse Publishing, 1991.

SYDNOR, W., *The Story of the REAL Prayer Book, 1549-1979.* Harrisburg, PA: Morehouse Publishing, 1989.

UNDERHILL, E., *Worship.* New York: Harper & Row, Publishers, 1937.

WEBBER, R. E., *Liturgical Evangelism.* Harrisburg, PA: Morehouse Publishing, 1992.

Chapter V

The Church's Lore

THE CHURCH YEAR

Just as there is a civil calendar with its seasons and holidays, so also there is an ecclesiastical calendar. The ecclesiastical year begins with Advent Sunday (the fourth Sunday before Christmas) and comprises seven seasons: Advent (a penitential season in preparation both for Christmas and the coming of Christ as Judge); Christmas (celebrating the birth of our Lord); Epiphany (celebrating our Lord's manifestation to all nations as typified in the coming of the Wise Men and in His baptism); Lent (a penitential season in preparation for Easter); Holy Week (commemorating our Lord's death and burial and the events immediately preceding); Easter (celebrating the resurrection of our Lord, and including in its Great Fifty Days Ascensiontide (celebrating the universalization of His ministry) and the Day of Pentecost (celebrating the outpouring of the Holy Spirit upon the disciples); and the Season after Pentecost (commemorating the Spirit's leading and teaching the Church thereafter).

Easter is the Christian Passover, commemorating God's delivering His new Israel, the Christian Church, through Christ out of the bondage to sin and death, as He delivered the old Israel through Moses from their bondage to the Egyptians. Pentecost means "fiftieth" in Greek, and is the ancient Jewish Feast of Weeks (seven weeks from the Passover), commemorating in later times the giving of the Law to Moses on Mount Sinai. Formerly in English-speaking countries it was called Whitsunday. It is considered to be the birthday of the Church, when the disciples became alive through the Holy Spirit and went forth to preach the Gospel. The time and length of many of these seasons are dependent upon the date of Easter, which is always the first Sunday after the full moon (computed according to an ancient reckoning) occurring after March 21st.

There are three kinds of days in the ecclesiastical year, all beginning with the letter *f:* feasts, fasts, and ferias. A feast is a day of rejoicing, a fast is a day of penitence and abstention in varying measure from food, and a feria is an ordinary day which is neither a feast nor a fast. Feasts may be either movable or immovable. All Sundays of the year are feasts, being commemorations of the resurrection of our Lord, which occurred on the first day of the week.

Fasts are divided into two kinds: days of strict fasting and days when it is customary to abstain from certain kinds of foods. Of the first class there are only two days observed in the Episcopal Church: Ash Wednesday (the first day of Lent) and Good Friday (the day on which our Lord was crucified). On them it is generally customary to abstain from all food and drink from the midnight preceding until three o'clock in the afternoon, and then only to partake of such food as is necessary, and in

no case to eat meat or drink liquor. On fast days of the
second class it is usually customary to abstain from eating
meat, and from having elaborate meals, and from giving
parties or entertainments. Fasting, when religiously and
sensibly used, can become an effective means of self-
discipline which will bear spiritual fruit.

Christians are expected to keep appropriately the
Church's feasts and fasts. They are expected to attend
divine worship every Sunday and on the great feasts occurring during the week (Christmas, Epiphany, Ascension, All Saints, Thanksgiving), and on such other holy
days as they are able. They are expected to observe the
fast days with appropriate acts of penitence, to refrain
from work on Good Friday, and to attend Church on that
day. On Christmas, Easter, and Pentecost, after due
preparation, they are expected to make Communion, and
to receive the Sacrament throughout the rest of the year
with such frequency as is spiritually helpful.

During Advent Christians are expected to make some
special religious effort in preparation for Christmas. It is
an excellent time to read through one of the Gospels and
to undertake some form of Christian social service. Lent
is not so much a time for giving up things as it is of taking on additional religious activity. It often happens that
in order to assume extra spiritual activities it is necessary
to cease spending time and money on personal pleasures;
but it is a silly thing merely to give up eating candy
without contributing the money so saved to charity, or
not to go to the theatre without at the same time attending extra Lenten services. The usual observance of Lent
includes not attending or giving formal social parties;
some abstinence in the matter of food and drink; frequent
attendance at church services, extra Bible reading, and
some extra form of Christian service activity.

Each of the seasons and holy days has a color appropriate to its meaning, taken from the five common ecclesiastical colors: white, purple, green, red, and black. White is the color of joy, and is used on the great feasts such as Christmas and Easter, and on the feasts of saints who were not martyrs. It is used also at baptisms, confirmations, marriages, and ordinations. Purple is the color of penitence, and is used during Advent and Lent. Green is the color of nature, and is used on the ordinary Sundays and ferias after Epiphany and Pentecost. Red is the color of blood and flame, and is used on the feasts of martyrs and on Pentecost (because of the fiery tongues which were thought to have alighted on the disciples' heads). Black is the color of mourning, and is used on Good Friday and at burials and requiems.

CHURCH BUILDINGS

The plan of a church building may be seen at its best in the Gothic cathedral. A cathedral is the mother church of a diocese in which the bishop has his *cathedra* or throne. It is divided into three main parts: the nave (or ship of salvation) in which the people sit, the choir in which the singers and ministers sit, and the sanctuary in which the high altar stands. The choir and sanctuary together form the chancel, which is divided from the nave by the chancel rail, or else by a screen. This is called a rood-screen if it bears upon it a rood (an old Anglo-Saxon word for "cross"). The sanctuary is divided from the choir by the communion or altar rail. The altar is a constant reminder that the way of sacrifice is the only means of approach to God. Free-standing table altars, with only one candlestick on each end, with or without drapery adornment, and behind which the celebrant may face the people at the Eucharist, have become quite popular since the Liturgical Movement. There is generally a large hanging cross above the altar, or else behind it. Formerly most altars were against the eastern wall, behind which was a stone or wooden reredos, often elaborately carved, or hanging curtains known as a dossal. Sometimes curtains, called riddels, extend out on both sides of the altar. The rear portion of the altar is often raised, forming a retable upon which the cross, candles, and flower vases are usually placed. In the Episcopal Church at each end of the retable is generally a tall candlestick. These are known as eucharistic lights because they are lighted only at the celebration of the Eucharist. However, in churches with only the two candles, they are often lighted at all services. In the center stands a cross of various designs. If it bears upon it a *corpus,* or figure of our Lord, it is known as a crucifix. There may be also on either side of the cross various candlesticks, often seven-branched, known as office lights, which are lighted at the other services besides Holy Communion. The top of the altar is generally marked with five crosses, commemorating the five wounds of our Lord, and at the time of the Eucharist bears a clean white cloth upon it.

In the choir the choristers sit in choir stalls and the clergy in clergy stalls, while in the nave the people sit in pews or else on what are known as cathedral chairs. In the sanctuary on the Gospel side is placed a seat for the bishop and on the Epistle side, as a rule, three seats, or *sedilia,* for the clergy. Near to the *sedilia* on the sanctuary wall is generally a small shelf or niche known as the credence table, upon which the bread-box and the cruets of wine and water for the Communion Service are placed.

In every church there is a baptismal font, often placed near the door to signify that Baptism is the entrance to the Church. As Baptism is symbolically the resurrection to a new life, fonts are often octagonal in shape because there are eight accounts of resurrections in the Bible.

Cathedrals are as a rule cruciform, that is, built in the shape of a cross, and with the high altar at the eastern end (orientated) facing towards Jerusalem, where it was believed that the second coming of the Lord would occur, but in all likelihood placed there rather to get the morning light. The arms of the cross are known as the transepts, the nave forming the shaft, the crossing the intersection, and the apse the head of the shaft of the cross. Within the apse is the chancel, and often around the chancel there is an aisle known as an ambulatory, off of which there may be various chapels, known as apsidal chapels, the one directly behind the high altar generally being dedicated to the Virgin and known as the Lady Chapel. Along the side aisles of the nave are often placed various chapels, and at its western end there is the narthex or vestibule. Ordinarily parish churches conform to a large extent to this same arrangement, being divided into the same three parts of nave, choir and sanctuary, although not always cruciform in shape.

CHURCH SYMBOLISM

There are various symbols found in the carving and glass of churches which have come throughout the ages to stand for certain great Christian truths. The symbols of the Godhead are many, the principal ones being the triangle and trefoil representing the Trinity, the circle the eternity of God, the hand the power of God the Father, and the dove God the Holy Spirit.

The symbols of our Lord are numerous, in addition to the obvious symbols of His birth, such as the star, and of His passion, such as the cross, the whipping-post, the crown of thorns, and the nails. The A and Ω (Alpha and Omega, the first and last letters of the Greek alphabet) represent Him as the beginning and end of all things. The IHΣ (Iota Eta Sigma) is the first three Greek letters of His Name Jesus. They also represent the Latin *Iesus Hominum Salvator* (Jesus Savior of Men). The Chi Rho (XP) stands for Christ, being the first two Greek letters of that name. The pelican, which was supposed to feed its young with its own blood, stands for our Lord feeding people in the Holy Communion with His Body and Blood. The phoenix, which rose again from its own ashes, symbolizes the resurrection of our Lord. He is also frequently pictured as the Good Shepherd and as the *Agnus Dei,* the Lamb of God, the lamb frequently holding a pennon. The fish was an early symbol for Christ as I X Θ Τ Σ, the word for fish in Greek, being regarded as composed of the first letters of the phrase which in English means, "Jesus Christ, God's Son, Savior." The vine symbolizes our Lord's reference to Himself as the true Vine (John 15:1).

The evangelists, as a rule, are pictured holding a book, and with their own appropriate symbols (taken from Ezekiel 1:10 and Revelation 4:7) beside them: the man for St. Matthew; the winged lion for St. Mark; the ox for St. Luke; and the eagle for St. John. Martyrs are generally represented with the instrument of their martyrdom; St. Paul, for instance, being pictured with a sword. Builders of cathedrals often hold a model of the cathedral in their hands. Bishops generally wear cope and mitre and hold a crosier, and archbishops a cross with a small crossbar above the usual crossbeam. St. Peter as a rule carriers the two keys, the golden key of heaven and the iron key of hell.

The cross also, as well as the shield, represents faith, the anchor hope, and the heart charity or love. The crown and the palm represent the victory of the saints. The cross and the crown together symbolize the fact that in order to wear the crown it is necessary to bear the cross.

Since 1940 the Episcopal Church has had its own flag, whose colors are red, white, and blue, signifying that it is American. The St. George's cross (a red cross on a white field) commemorates its descent from the Church of England, whose flag is just like that. The nine white cross crosslets (betokening the nine original American dioceses), arranged in the form of a St. Andrew's cross (testifying that our first bishop was consecrated in Scotland), are in a canton of blue.

VESTMENTS

The clergy and choir members and acolytes wear over their ordinary clothing a long gown with sleeves known as a cassock. Its color is generally black, although in cathedral churches it is often purple (the episcopal color), and acolytes often wear red. At the choir offices (Morning and Evening Prayer) over this the clergy wear a surplice, a white garment reaching as a rule to the knees. Choir members and servers sometimes wear a shorter overgarment known as a cotta. Many of the clergy wear hoods, which signify various academic degrees conferred by educational institutions, and which vary in size, shape, and color in accordance with the particular degree, faculty, and institution. Over this at choir offices clergy generally wear a black scarf, often called a tippet. At sacramental services clergy wear stoles, differing in color according to the nature of the service, or, at the Eucharist, according to the day of the church year.

Bishops wear over their cassocks, often purple in color, a white garment known as a rochet, and over this a black silk garment (sometimes red), with white lawn sleeves and cuffs, known as a chimere. They often wear hoods and scarves.

At the services of the Holy Communion some clergy wear the so-called eucharistic vestments over their cassocks. These consist of the amice or large white collar; the alb, a long white gown with sleeves covering the cassock; the cincture or girdle; the stole crossed over their breast (unless a bishop, who wears his hanging straight down); and over all the chasuble (sometimes of linen, but generally of silk of the color of the day), a handsomely embroidered garment. Other clergy wear simply the customary cassock, surplice, and stole.

Sometimes bishops and other clergy in processions wear copes, which are elaborately embroidered silk capes. Bishops traditionally wear mitres on ceremonial occasions and carry, or have carried before them, their pastoral staff or crosier, which is symbolic of their office of chief shepherd of God's flock, the Church.

COMMUNION LINEN AND VESSELS

The altar at a celebration of the Holy Communion is traditionally covered with three cloths. The first is the cere cloth covering the top of the altar. Over this is placed a larger white cloth and over that the white cloth prescribed by the Prayer Book rubric, generally marked with five Greek crosses.

The vessels used in administering the Holy Communion are a round plate of precious metal called a paten on which the bread, generally in the form of wafers, is placed, and a cup or chalice of like precious metal for the wine. These are placed upon the altar on the corporal, a small square of white linen placed upon the altar cloth. The other Communion linens are a pall (a stiffened square of linen to cover the chalice), a purificator for wiping the chalice dry after the cleansing or ablutions, and sometimes a linen chalice veil. The chalice and paten are brought to the altar covered by a silk veil of the color of the day on top of which rests the burse, a square pocket made of the silk of the color of the day containing the corporal. On the credence table are the two cruets of wine and water and the bread-box or ciborium.

CHURCH CUSTOMS

It is customary on entering an Episcopal church to go quietly to one's seat and kneel and say a prayer, in which one prays for the Church, for those who minister there, for those who worship there, and for oneself that one may be strengthened and refreshed through one's worship. During the service there is a threefold general rule of posture: Sit for instruction, stand for praise, kneel for prayer. Consequently, one sits for the lessons, the announcements, the sermon, and for the Epistle in the Communion Service. One stands for the hymns, Psalms, canticles, the Creed, and, as a special mark of respect, for the Gospel in the Eucharist. One kneels, not hunches, for most of the prayers, the confession and absolution, and the blessing. One is now, however, allowed to stand for many prayers, as well as for the blessing. Nevertheless, it is courteous to follow the parish practice where one is worshipping.

The priest, as the representative of our Lord, stands when giving the absolution and the blessing. He or she faces the altar for the Creed and sometimes for direct ascriptions of praise to God, such as the *Gloria Patri.*

Many Christians, in accordance with Philippians 2:10 and as an act of reparation for the blasphemous use of our Lord's Name, bow their heads not only in the Creeds at the mention of "Jesus," but also whenever else it is spoken. People also often bow their heads at any ascription to the Trinity, such as "Glory be to the Father, and to the Son, and to the Holy Ghost," or "Praise Father, Son, and Holy Ghost," or "Holy, Holy, Holy, Lord God of hosts." Many people bow their heads to the cross, when passing before the altar or when the cross is carried in procession past them, or when they enter or leave their pew, just as people salute the flag when carried in procession, or members of the English House of Lords bow to the throne when passing it.

There are members of the Episcopal Church who like to show special reverence to our Lord's Presence in the Eucharist by genuflecting, that is, kneeling on their right knee, when the consecrated Bread and Wine are on the altar. They also like vividly to recall to themselves our Lord's Passion, and, consequently, often make the sign of the cross, touching with their right hand their forehead, breastbone, left shoulder, right shoulder. This is commonly done at the beginning and end of their private prayers, at the absolution, at the end of the creeds, at the beginning of the *Magnificat,* at the end of the

Gloria in excelsis, before the reception of the elements of the Holy Communion, at the blessing, and at grace before and after meals.

During the actual ceremonies of Baptism, Confirmation, and Marriage the congregation stands, and during the eucharistic part of these services it conducts itself as at any other Eucharist. At burials the congregation is supposed to take part in the service and to stand, sit, and kneel as it would at any other church service, even when it is held at home or in some secular building. When the committal is said indoors in connection with the rest of the service, the congregation should stand. At the end of the Burial Service it is customary for those present to remain in their places until the pallbearers and chief mourners have left the church.

Whenever candles are lighted upon the altar or in the sanctuary the congregation is expected to remain quietly at its private prayers after the service until the last candle is extinguished. Before leaving the church one should kneel down and say a prayer asking God to bless the service that it may bring forth fruit in one's life, and that He may strengthen and protect those present and all others of His children; and, if one has received the Holy Communion, a special act of thanksgiving should be made for the benefits which have been received through participation in it.

The person who is to receive Holy Communion should come quietly to the communion rail; kneel down when there is room; and, with the right hand crossed over the left and raised level with the breast, receive the sacred Host into the open palm of the right hand and convey it to the mouth without handling it, and consume it without touching it with the teeth. When the minister comes with the chalice, the communicant should, with head erect, guide the chalice to the lips by gently taking hold of the foot, not the rim, with the right hand. It is sufficient that the Sacred Wine touch the lips. The Communion is not an act of eating or drinking, but of spiritual communion through the consecrated Bread and Wine. Gloves should be removed and veils lifted before approaching the communion rail. If there are only a few people at the rail, it is usual to wait until all have been communicated before returning to one's seat; but if there are people waiting, it is customary to return as soon as the minister administering the chalice has communicated the second person beyond one, or the group with which one came to the communion rail.

BOOKS FOR FURTHER READING

BOOTY, J. E., *What Makes Us Episcopalians?* Harrisburg, PA: Morehouse Publishing, 1982.

BRADNER, J., *Symbols of Church Seasons and Days.* Harrisburg, PA: Morehouse Publishing, 1977.

FERGUSON, G. W., *Signs and Symbols in Christian Art*, 2nd ed. New York: Oxford University Press, 1966.

POST, W. E., *Saints, Signs, and Symbols*, 2nd ed. Harrisburg, PA: Morehouse Publishing, 1974.

STALEY, V., *The Catholic Religion, A Manual of Instruction for Members of the Anglican Communion.* Harrisburg, PA: Morehouse Publishing, 1983.

WILSON, F. E., *Faith and Practice*, rev. ed. Harrisburg, PA: Morehouse Publishing, 1989.

Chapter VI

The Church's Prayer Life

A Christian is etymologically one who belongs to Christ — one who has given his life to Him in Baptism to be used and to be made according as He wills. Consequently, it is necessary to be in communication with God in order both to find out what God would have one do with one's life, and to receive the divine power and strength without which the task can not be accomplished. Prayer is the means by which both of these are done.

To the popular mind, prayer is a series of petitions recited to God attempting to bend His will to that of the person praying, and which God is honor-bound to fulfill if it is "in accordance with His will." But prayer is no such thing at all! Since God has conferred free will upon His creatures it is no longer possible for Him to accomplish anything with or through them without their consent. No matter how insistently God may knock at the door of one's heart, that door can only be opened from within by oneself. And prayer is the means by which one voluntarily makes contact with the wisdom and power of God and opens up the channels through which the divine grace may flow into one's life. Prayer is, then, not an attempt to conform God to one's scheme of things, but the means of adjusting one's life to God's plan.

Now prayer is something independent of time, place, or bodily position, and the lives of the greatest saints have been "one long-continued prayer"; but with the ordinary man and woman it helps, at first, to have regular times of praying, and to find a quiet place where one can be alone and unobserved, and where one can assume a kneeling posture. The large majority of Christians are accustomed to say their prayers at night before going to bed. By that they generally mean reciting the Lord's Prayer and some other prayers they have learned along with a list of people to be blessed and protected. But, as can be seen, this is a very inadequate conception of prayer, and the ending of the day is not nearly so appropriate a time as the beginning.

For the ordinary Christian who has not advanced far in the art of prayer some such scheme as the following should prove helpful. In the morning after being fully washed and dressed, kneel down quietly by oneself and keep first of all a minute of silence or waiting, and then begin to make acts of recollection. By that is meant to call to mind the kind of God to whom one is speaking. "O God of love, who dost love me with a greater love than I can either know or understand." "O heavenly Father, who dost will only that which is good for all Thy children," etc. This should be followed by an act of dedication of one's life to God for that day, a consecration of one's thoughts and words and deeds to His service. Then the events of the day as known should be gone over with God, the duties and the people with whom one will come into contact should be talked over with Him, and His guidance sought as to what is best to do, and the strength requested to follow His guidance. And after this come intercessions, the people and causes which one carries in one's heart and has on one's mind. Afterwards one's personal needs of spiritual development should be brought before God and definite acts of righteousness along those lines determined upon for that day. Here one should make an oblation, a definite offering of oneself to God to be used in His service on that day — a willingness to let God guide and direct one as He sees fit. And then should come the listening-time of prayer, the time when one is still and God speaks, the most important time of all prayer. It is then that God will not only guide one in the events confronting one that day, but will suggest ways in which the person praying can personally help the people and causes for which intercession has been made, and by which he or she can also attain the spiritual progress for which they have petitioned.

Before each meal one should ask God's blessing on His gifts of food, and after each meal thank Him for those gifts. In the modern world this may often have to be done silently and unobtrusively, but there is no reason for its omission. Christians will also learn throughout the day to turn to God in short silent prayer or thanksgiving, as the occasion arises. Many pause at noon each day to recollect not only the morning past, but the afternoon and evening to come, and to pray for the spread of God's Kingdom in the world.

The prayers at night also should begin with a silence, and then acts of recollection. This should be followed by a review of one's thoughts, words, and actions during the day in the light of God's Presence and a confession of one's sins and failings before Him. The confession should be definite and specific, and should avoid any attempt to excuse oneself. God Himself knows better than any person what allowances should be made. Next should come a recital of the things for which one has to be thankful throughout the day, and an outpouring of the heart in gratitude to God for His many blessings. It should not be forgotten that gratitude to God should be just as great for the continuing blessings of life, such as shelter, food, clothing, health, parents, friends as for any special or unusual attainments, protection, or gifts of that one day. Afterwards should come intercessions, and as they increase in number, it is sometimes well to group them around various large topics, and to assign a particular day to each. These should naturally include not only those who pray for one, but also all for whom one ought to pray, as well as all those who have no one to pray for them. Following this one's own needs should be made known, not to inform God, but to dedicate one's will to Him that He may aid one. Then one ends with a commendation of oneself and all people to His love, followed by an ascription of praise to Him for His goodness and mercy and inestimable love and His very Being. Last of all a moment or so should be spent in adoration, vocal or silent, before one says *Amen,* so be it. Then one should turn to God to listen to what He has to say in the way of guidance and encouragement.

Prayer, when conceived in such terms, can become an occasion of joyous fellowship with One we love, and the means whereby our lives grow like unto His and we meet the problems of life in His strength and look out upon the world through His all-loving eyes. Perseverance in prayer is the measure of our real desire for that for which we pray.

What has been said, of course, applies equally to public prayer; only there the expressions must be more general and more formal in order to cover the needs and desires of all sorts and conditions of humanity. Public prayer is a corporate expression of the Church's dependence upon God, a dedication of the lives of its members both individually and collectively to His service, and an opening up of the corporate mind and life of the Christian community, that it may be filled with His wisdom and supplied with His strength; as well as a knitting of people together in the fellowship of the one Spirit.

THE LORD'S PRAYER

In answer to a request of His disciples our Lord gave them a model prayer which soon became known as the Lord's Prayer, and has been in constant use ever since. In its original Aramaic form it probably ran something like this: "Father, hallowed be Thy Name, Thy Kingdom come. Give us our bread day by day. And forgive us our sins, as we also forgive everyone who sins against us. And let us not yield to temptation." It was translated into Greek and expanded and altered slightly in usage, and a doxology appended to it. In its present form it is divided into four parts: the address; petitions concerning God; petitions concerning humanity; and the doxology.

The Lord's Prayer is found in the Bible in two variant forms: Matthew 6:9—13 and Luke 11:2—4. The version used in the Prayer Book is a very early one, dating from before the sixteenth-century English translation of the Bible. The American Prayer Book has slightly modernized the phraseology.

Our Father. In these two words are contained two of the great doctrines of Christianity: the Fatherhood of God and the "Brotherhood of Man." The Lord's Prayer is addressed to a God who, our Lord taught us, is a loving

Father. One must not, however, think of God as solely masculine. Certainly there is embraced within the Godhead all of those great qualities which we associate with the term motherhood (*cf.* Isaiah 66:13). The prayer is an unselfish one throughout; it asks that all may share in that which is petitioned.

Who art in heaven. Heaven is not a locality but a state of life — the state of life in which God dwells, the quality of life which emanates from and surrounds His Presence. Although we stand in the intimate relationship to God of child to parent, yet He is at the same time above and beyond us. This phrase lifts our thoughts from the temporal to the eternal, from the material to the spiritual.

Hallowed be thy Name. Thy kingdom come. Thy will be done, On earth as it is in heaven. These three clauses go together, and the phrase "on earth as it is in heaven" goes with each of them. When God's will is done, then is His Kingdom or rule come in that individual, and His Name held holy. "Name" in Hebrew usage is a metonym for God. "Hallowed" means to be treated as holy or sacred. "Kingdom" really means here "kingship," or "rule," or "reign." So the clauses taken together are a petition that God's will may be done and so His rule established and He Himself properly worshipped by faithful service. It should be noted that the first concern of the Lord's Prayer is with God, His worship, rule, and purposes. He comes before all else.

Give us this day our daily bread. The exact meaning of the Greek word translated "daily" is not certain, but it probably means "for the morrow." The clause is a petition that each day we may be given the food for our next meal. It is a request for the necessities of life as they are actually needed, not for a superfluity or for luxuries. It asks God that all may be supplied alike with these necessities. Christians who truly pray this prayer will do their part to see that all are. They will not desire more for themselves than others, nor more than is actually necessary, realizing that one's needs are quite different from one's desires. Furthermore, this petition acknowledges our dependence upon God who is the Giver of all good gifts. It marks the beginning of the third section of the prayer.

And forgive us our trespasses, As we forgive those who trespass against us. A more literal translation of the Greek, which is found in the Authorized Version of the Bible, runs: "And forgive us our debts, as we forgive our debtors." Both of these mean: "And forgive us our sins as we forgive those who sin against us." In the first case sin is looked upon as a trespass into forbidden territory; in the second, which is a common Jewish view, we are looked upon as owing God perfect obedience, and every time we disobey Him we are in debt to God for that obedience which we did not pay. The petition is a plea for mercy, but at the same time it is recognized that God cannot forgive us until we forgive our brothers and sisters, for God only forgives us when we repent, and as long as we are nourishing ill in our hearts toward someone else, we are not repentant. We are neither required nor expected to forgive others until they do repent. What is required is the willingness to forgive others upon their repentance, an absence of all thought of revenge, and an attitude of loving goodwill towards all at all times.

And lead us not into temptation. This clause has puzzled interpreters from the earliest times, because it is only through meeting and overcoming temptation that we are able to become good, the Christian character built-up, and righteousness attained. Many think that the Greek is a mistranslation of the original Aramaic spoken by our Lord and that the clause should read: "And let us not yield to temptation." A few, less probably, consider it a petition to be delivered from the fiery trial and woes which at that time were expected to precede the end of the world. Others, who accept the words as they stand, take them closely with the following words and paraphrase in some such way as this: "Knowing we are weak, lead us not into temptation, lest we fall; but if we do meet with temptation, strengthen us so that we are delivered from falling into evil."

But deliver us from evil. Or perhaps from the evil one or devil. Christians at that time believed in evil as well as good spirits. Many modern Christians do not believe in a personal devil, but they do just as earnestly pray that all may be delivered from both moral and physical evil. The two clauses together form a petition for spiritual strength. This is the original ending of the Lord's Prayer, and at this point it ends in the Roman Church, and sometimes in our own Prayer Book when used on penitential and sorrowful occasions.

For thine is the kingdom, and the power, and the glory, forever and ever. Amen. This is a doxology, or ascription of praise to the Deity, added to the prayer by the early Church, just as still today such a doxology is added to the end when the Psalms or canticles are said. Here it is our acknowledgment that God's rule, power, and praise are eternal. "Amen" is a Hebrew word meaning "so be it." It is the congregation's solemn asseveration that they earnestly pray that the prayers may be granted which not only they themselves say, but which also the minister says for them. One should always audibly say "Amen" at the end of every prayer, for the worship of the Episcopal Church is congregational, and this marks the participation of the congregation in those prayers said for them by the person representing them, called the parson.

The Lord's Prayer was given as a model, not as a magical formula, and due to its great familiarity and frequent use, it is necessary for all to say it slowly, thoughtfully, and reverently in order to make its petitions one's own desires. It is well in saying it privately to pause after each clause and to consider its significance for the specific problems of one's own life and that of the world around one. By so doing one more fully enters into the mind of the Lord, and grows into closer communion with the God whom He taught His disciples to call their Father.

BOOKS FOR FURTHER READING

BARCLAY, W., *Prayers For Young People.* Nashville, TN: Abingdon, 1993.

FROST, B., *The Art of Mental Prayer.* Harrisburg, PA: Morehouse Publishing, 1988.

HOSMER, R. and JONES, A., *Living in the Spirit.* San Francisco: HarperSF, 1985.

LEWIS, C. S., *The Joyful Christian.* New York: Macmillan, 1984.

_____, *Letters to Malcolm: Chiefly on Prayer.* New York: Harbrace, 1973.

MORGAN, H., ed., *Approaches to Prayer, A Resource Book for Groups and Individuals.* Harrisburg, PA: Morehouse Publishing, 1991.

SHEPHERD, M. H., Jr., *A Companion of Prayer for Daily Living.* Harrisburg, PA: Morehouse Publishing, 1978.

UNDERHILL, E., *Abba.* Harrisburg, PA: Morehouse Publishing, 1982.

_____, *Concerning the Inner Life.* New York: E. P. Dutton & Co., 1927.

_____, *Life as Prayer: And Other Papers of Evelyn Underhill.* Harrisburg, PA: Morehouse Publishing, 1991.

_____, *The Spiritual Life.* Harrisburg, PA: Morehouse Publishing, 1955.

Forward Day-by-Day. Cincinnati: Forward Movement Publications.

Chapter VII

The Church's Moral Law

The Church's moral law is summed up in the great saying of our Lord in which He combined two well-known verses from the Jewish Law — Deuteronomy 6:5 and Leviticus 19:18: "Thou shalt love the Lord thy God with all thy heart, and with all thy soul, and with all thy mind. This is the first and great commandment. And the second is like unto it. Thou shalt love thy neighbor as thyself. On these two commandments hang all the law and the prophets" (Matthew 22:37—40).

All Christian moral and religious teaching is but a commentary on these two fundamental principles that we are called upon to love God and to love our brothers and sisters. One is called upon above all to love God and to place Him first, but it is impossible to love God without loving one's brothers and sisters at the same time.

This means that the standard of moral judgment of our thoughts, words, and deeds is whether or not they are loving. No thought, word, or action which cannot fulfill that qualification is Christian. Our Lord left no detailed enactments for the government of human life, but simply these fundamental principles which He gave us to apply ourselves to the particular problem which we meet in the daily life of our own generation. He imparted not so much a set of laws for living, as a responsibility towards life.

It has often been thought that the Ten Commandments are the rules of Christian conduct. As a matter of fact they are even below the level of the best Jewish moral teaching, for they represent the Jewish ethical standards of about the seventh century B.C. The Jews originally believed that they were given by God to Moses on Mount Sinai, but in reality they date from various periods, mostly later than the time of Moses. It is only by fulfilling them, that is, filling them full of Christian meaning, that they become valuable for Christian use today. Our Lord did this when He spoke of a person being angry at another, that is, wishing him harm, as breaking the sixth commandment; or a person planning in his mind to have intercourse with a woman not his wife, as breaking the seventh commandment. A person who breaks any of the commandments (except the fourth) is certainly sinning grievously, but one could keep all of them and yet be very far from being a Christian. They are not Christianly invalid, but Christianly insufficient.

The Ten Commandments are found in slightly variant forms in two places in the Bible: Exodus 20:3—17 and Deuteronomy 5:7—21. The version used in the Prayer Book is taken from Exodus according to the translation known as the Great Bible of 1540, instead of from the Authorized Version of 1611.

THE TEN COMMANDMENTS

I. *Thou shalt have none other gods but me.* This was

not originally a monotheistic statement, but a mono-
latrous; that is, there were other gods besides Yahweh
(the Name of Israel's God), but the Israelites were to
worship and have to do with only Him. Christians today
are to see that they have no other gods but God; that
parents, friends, wealth, social position, pleasures,
business, or worldly success do not take His place.

II. *Thou shalt not make to thyself any graven image,
nor the likeness of any thing that is in heaven above,
or in the earth beneath, or in the water under the earth;
thou shalt not bow down to them, nor worship them.*
This commandment forbids idolatry of all kinds: the making of images of the heavenly bodies, earthly creatures,
or marine life, and treating them as gods; and the wor-
shiping of images after they are made. Christians must
likewise see that they do not idolize material things or
creatures human or animal.

III. *Thou shalt not take the Name of the LORD thy God
in vain.* Originally forbade the use of Yahweh's Name
in an oath which was not kept, and warned that He would
punish any who did so; to a Christian it forbids, first of
all, blasphemy, which is the irreverent use of the Name
of God. Not only is blasphemy a sin itself, but far worse,
it indicates a frame of mind which is indifferent, if not
actually hostile, to God, and which has little or no love
for Him. A person does not use the names of those he
loves, parents or friends, in indecent or frivolous ways,
and neither do those who truly love God. Secondly it forbids cursing. Our Lord taught us to bless those who curse
us, and to wish all persons well. Cursing is not only evil
for the words used, but even more for the thought behind
the words. Thirdly, it forbids indecent conversation or
lewd jokes of any sort. Fourthly, it forbids profanity.
There are however, certain expressions which are more

unconventional than sinful. Still, a Christian seeks never to give offense, and so he will not use them as long as social convention is against them.

IV. *Remember that thou keep holy the Sabbath day.* This commandment refers to the time from sundown Friday to sundown Saturday but its application was transferred to the Christian Sunday or first day of the week. Every day is sacred to God. Anything which is right to do on Monday is also right, although not always advisable, to do on Sunday; and anything which is wrong to do on Sunday is wrong to do on any other day of the week. With God there is no demand for a blue Sabbath. However, Christians who do not find it convenient to attend the daily worship of God in those churches which have it, are expected to attend His worship on Sunday and to support the services of His Church. Furthermore, Christians who have a day of rest for themselves will seek to see that others have one as well. Moreover most Christians, although God has never commanded it, will wish to show special reverence to the day of our Lord's resurrection by voluntarily refraining from certain activities which they do on other days. Even though dancing, card playing, parties, athletics, the theatre, amusements, and business are not sinful on Sunday, yet most Christians will refrain from participating in them on that day as a voluntary offering of respect on their part to God.

V. *Honor thy father and thy mother.* Respect for one's parents and elders was a cardinal requirement of Judaism. Courtesy is still today a fundamental Christian virtue, and it is nowhere more truly shown than to one's parents. Furthermore, because a ruler has from ancient times been regarded as the father of his people, obedience to lawful authority is also considered enjoined by this commandment.

VI. *Thou shalt do no murder.* This commandment, as our Lord explained, forbids, from a Christian point of view, the wishing or doing of harm in any way to anyone. It forbids one not only to take another's physical life, unless legally ordered as in execution, a just war, or police protection, but also to hinder or thwart anyone in the full enjoyment of the spiritual life which God intends us to have.

VII. *Thou shalt not commit adultery.* Adultery is voluntary sexual intercourse between a man and a woman, when one or both of them are married to someone else. In its primitive form it applied only to a married woman, and was considered a violation of her husband's property right. Adultery is also a violation of the marriage vows in the Prayer Book. From the traditional Christian point of view this commandment has been taken to forbid sexual impurity of any kind in deed, word, and thought (*cf.* Matthew 5:27,28), and all sexual intercourse outside of marriage.

This traditional attitude towards sex, based on the Bible, is under strong ethical challenge today. Many modern moral theologians would hold views more or less similar to what follows. Sex is given for our enjoyment and ought to be both creative and integrative, as well as under planned circumstances for the procreation of children. Although a sexual act as such is not of itself sinful, it can become so by the circumstances accompanying it; and also by an obsession with it which shuts out God and the greater welfare of the community. Masturbation is not a sin and in moderation not at all harmful. Heterosexual intercourse between unmarried persons (fornication), with mutual consent and proper precautions against procreation and disease, is a private matter. This applies also to homosexual intercourse between mature consentient persons. Homosexuality itself is neither a sin nor a disease, but a condition for which the person himself is in no wise responsible.

In all sexual actions a Christian is required to be loving, and to treat others as persons, and not to use them as things; to regard them as ends, and not means. This is particularly so within the marriage bond. A Christian should dedicate his or her sexuality, as well as his or her personality, to the guidance and keeping of God.

VIII. *Thou shalt not steal.* This forbids the unlawful appropriation of that which is not one's own. It includes not only theft, but embezzlement, extortion, fraudulent appropriation of all kinds, borrowing and not returning, the wasting of other people's time, and the stealing of their good name and reputation.

IX. *Thou shalt not bear false witness against thy neighbor.* From a Christian point of view this forbids dishonesty of all kinds. To be dishonest is not to say what is not so, a thing which all have, through ignorance, been continually doing from the very beginning, but to attempt to deceive for unworthy motives. It is deception for one's own advantage, or for malicious purposes, that is forbidden.

X. *Thou shalt not covet.* From an ethical point of view this is the most advanced of all the commandments, as it has chiefly to do with an interior state of mind. Coveting means to want something for yourself which would deprive someone else of it. It is not wrong of itself to want an automobile just like that of Mr. X so that you both have one; but it is wrong to want Mr. X's automobile so that you will have it and he will not.

As is easily seen, these Ten Commandments are chiefly negative; they deal with only a few sins, and those chiefly individualistic, and they have nothing to say about the positive duties of people, or of their collective obligations, or social sins. They are by all means to be observed, but, much more than that, the Christian is to seek to live in communion with God, which means to become morally like unto Him, and that requires one to wish all people well. A Christian, furthermore, is humble, forgetting self and remembering God. And at all times and in all places we are called upon to put God first, other people second, and ourselves last. The priority in regard to other people for those unmarried runs: parents, relatives, friends, near neighbors, etc. For the married: spouse, children, parents, etc.

Some people seem to think that Jewish and Christian morality is summed up in the so-called Golden Rule: "Therefore all things whatsoever ye would that men should do to you, do ye even so to them: for this is the law and the prophets" (Matthew 7:12; cf. Luke 6:31). However the statement is too subjective and too superficial to be a good norm for ethical conduct. It works better in generalities (if you wish to have kindness shown you, be kind to other people) than in specifics (if you want someone to bring you a bowl of tripe, do not bring him one, unless you know that he likes it).

The Christian virtues are more properly found in such sayings as that of St. Paul (Galatians 5:22,23): "The fruit of the Spirit is love, joy, peace, longsuffering, gentleness, goodness, faith, meekness, temperance"; and of our Lord, especially in the Sermon on the Mount. The so-called Beatitudes, contained therein (Matthew 5:3—10) are an excellent catalogue of Christian virtues, and testify to the spiritual joy which is the characteristic of those who lead a Christian life.

THE BEATITUDES

Blessed are the poor in spirit: for theirs is the kingdom of heaven. Spiritually happy are the humble in mind: for in them does God reign. The first beatitude teaches the virtue of humility, one of the distinctive ethical characteristics of Christianity. It is only in the humble-minded that God can effect His will.

Blessed are they that mourn: for they shall be comforted. Spiritually happy are those who mourn because of evil; for they shall be strengthened to bear it. Those sensitive to the evil and sorrow of life will be given power to triumph over it.

Blessed are the meek: for they shall inherit the earth. Spiritually happy are those who are free from self-will and resentment: for they shall receive the good things which God has prepared for them. The first beatitude has to do primarily with one's attitude toward God; this one with one's attitude toward others. A not unhappy interpretation of "meek" here would be "good-natured."

Blessed are they which do hunger and thirst after righteousness: for they shall be filled. Spiritually happy are those who intensely desire to be righteous: for their wish will be satisfied. It is only those who really desire to become good who do become good.

Blessed are the merciful: for they shall obtain mercy. Spiritually happy are those who are compassionate and forbearing towards those in their power without claim upon them: for they will obtain like treatment from God. God forgives only those who themselves have a forgiving spirit.

Blessed are the pure in heart: for they shall see God. Spiritually happy are the single-minded: for so will they know God. It is only as one has a mind free from any defilement, corruption, or adulteration of evil that one is able completely to know God, to comprehend His will, to enter into full communion with Him. This beatitude is one of the most beautiful expressions of the goal of the Christian life.

Blessed are the peacemakers: for they shall be called the children of God. Spiritually happy are those who promote peace and prosperity among all: for in so doing they become like God. Peace, in Hebrew thought, not only denoted freedom from strife, but also included all the blessings of life. The peacemakers are those who promote the general welfare of humanity.

Blessed are they which are persecuted for righteousness' sake: for theirs is the kingdom of heaven. Spiritually happy are the righteous, even when persecuted: for in them God reigns. As long as one is in communion with God, as is the case when one does His will, nothing which the world can do to one matters. The joy of Christian martyrs has always been a great mystery to their tormentors, for they have no comprehension of what it means to live in God.

A Christian is bidden to practice virtue and to conquer sin not only in his or her own life, but in that of the world as well, particularly as it is now manifested in economic, social, and international relationships. One is called upon to perform the difficult task of hating sin, but loving sinners.

Sin has been variously defined. Theologically, it is disobedience to the will of God — anything which separates one from Him; morally, it is a failure to rise to the best that is in one — a choosing of the lower of two alternatives. Sins are traditionally divided into venial and mortal. Venial sins are those which are readily pardonable, while mortal sins are those of a grave nature which bring spiritual death to the soul. One can sin by omitting to do good, just as much as by doing evil.

Temptation, however, is not sin, no matter how frequently it may recur. But if one dwells with pleasure on the temptation in one's mind, or mentally performs the act to which one is tempted, although one does not do so by word or deed, one has nevertheless sinned, and in addition, done oneself psychological harm.

In order effectively to combat sin and to pursue virtue, it is necessary to have a rule of life and to keep it. The rule should be simple, but definite. It should include such things as regular times for praying, Bible reading, attending church, and receiving the Holy Communion. It should also have to do with one's daily habits, the spending of one's money, the use of one's leisure time, and Christian service activities in which one engages. But a rule of life is of itself not enough, for without the grace of perseverance little can be accomplished in this world. Consequently, a Christian must continually pray that God may grant perseverance unto the end in the high calling to which he or she has been dedicated of service and friendship with Christ in His work in the world.

Books for Further Reading

BRILL, E. H., *The Christian Moral Vision*. San Francisco: HarperSF, 1984.

ELMEN, P., ed., *The Anglican Moral Choice*. Harrisburg, PA: Morehouse Publishing, 1983.

KIRK, K. E., *The Vision of God*. Harrisburg, PA: Morehouse Publishing, 1991.

LEWIS, C. S., *A Grief Observed.* New York: Bantam, 1983.
_____, *The Problem of Pain.* New York: (Collier) Macmillan, 1978.
_____, *The Screwtape Letters.* New York: Macmillan, 1982; Bantam, 1984; and Dutton, 1988.
MACQUARRIE, J., *Dictionary of Christian Ethics.* Philadelphia: The Westminster Press, 1967.
SEDGWICK, T. and TURNER, P., *The Crisis in Moral Teaching in the Episcopal Church.* Harrisburg, PA: Morehouse Publishing, 1992.

Chapter VIII

The Church's Doctrine

The Church, forced to define its own beliefs by the emergence of heresies (false beliefs), wrought them out in ecumenical councils. The first, at Nicaea in 325, declared that Jesus was truly God; the second, at Constantinople in 381, declared that He had a human body, soul, and spirit and that the Holy Spirit was also divine. The third, at Ephesus in 431, stated that the incarnate Christ was a single Person, at once God and man. The fourth council, at Chalcedon in 451, rejected the idea that after the incarnation Christ had only one nature and affirmed that He was one Person in two natures united unconfusedly, unchangeably, indivisibly, and inseparably. It also promulgated the Nicene Creed.

THE DOCTRINE OF GOD

There is one God, uncreated and unchangeable, who has always existed and will always exist. His being is Spirit and His nature love, goodness, truth and beauty. He is all-powerful and all-wise and everywhere present. God by His very nature is self-limited so that He cannot do anything that is evil, absurd, or irrational.

Within the non-numerical unity of the Godhead there are three eternal distinctions, which we name Father, Son, and Holy Spirit, and together call the Trinity. (Holy Ghost is an older form of the name Holy Spirit, coming from the Anglo-Saxon *Halig Gast,* which means Holy Spirit.) These distinctions correspond to three eternal activities of God, those of creation, redemption, and sanctification. They are called Persons, but the word has a special technical meaning — the individual subsistence of a rational nature, not that generally given to it in ordinary conversation. It in no way implies that there are three distinctive personalities within the Godhead.

Possibly the best physical analogy as a help to the understanding of the Trinity is that of the one sun of this earth, which manifests itself as heat, light, and radiant energy. The best psychological analogy is St. Augustine's — the Lover, the Loved One, and the Love between them.

GOD THE FATHER

God the Father started the process by which the entire universe, including humanity is still being created. The Church is not committed to any theory of the exact way in which God creates, but only to the fact that He, and He alone, is Creator. Not only does God create, but He also sustains, provides for, watches over, and cares for that which He has created. This is known as the Providence of God. As a Father God rules His creation, and through discipline trains His children.

GOD THE SON

God the Son, the Second Person of the Trinity, became Man in the Person of Jesus Christ; God Himself starting the process by which He was born as a Man among men of the Virgin Mary. God became Man, in order that men might become like God. In the one Person of Jesus Christ there were both a complete divine and a complete human nature, united from then on without confusion, change, division, or separation, so that Jesus Christ is both perfect God and perfect Man. Through His life of perfect obedience to God's will culminating in His death upon the cross, He made atonement for the sins of all and showed them how they might break the power of sin and death over their lives and attain unto the righteousness of God.

Not only is Christ our Redeemer, but He is also the Revelation of God's Love, the Word or *Logos,* the Revealer of what God is like and what God wants His children to be like. In Him we see the divine life humanly lived and human life divinely lived. He is not only the Founder, but also the Head of the Christian Church, the Lord and Master to whom Christians owe obedience, love, and devotion.

GOD THE HOLY SPIRIT

If one were to translate God the Holy Spirit, the Third Person of the Trinity, into modern terms, the nearest equivalent would be the Mind of God. He it is who acts upon our minds, inspiring us to good, warning us from evil, giving us creative ability, guiding us, and leading us more and more into the knowledge of the truth and into the way of holiness; in other words He is the Sanctifier.

He is not conscience, which is merely one's mind acting in moral judgment, but He is the Educator of conscience.

THE DOCTRINE OF SALVATION

People are born with a free will of their own into an imperfect world with natural instincts which, when not controlled and sanctified, lead to sin. Sin is the conscious choosing of the worse of two alternatives, disobedience to the will of God, the failure to rise to the possibilities within one. Sin erects a barrier between us and God and hinders the free and full communication with Him in prayer. Through the atonement made on the cross by Christ it is possible for us to obtain the forgiveness of our sins when we repent and to obtain, besides, the power to conquer sin and live a life in communion with God, which is the real meaning of salvation. Salvation is being saved not only from sin, but also being saved unto righteousness. God in His infinite mercy treats those who pledge themselves to Him in baptism and seriously attempt to live according to His will as saved, although they have not as yet attained that state of full surrender and communion with Him. This is what is called in theological language justification by faith. Salvation is a present fact, and something which can always be gained or lost as long as one has free will.

THE DOCTRINE OF EVIL

Philosophers of various periods, religions, and climes have grappled with the problem of evil and its reconciliation with the belief in an all-powerful God who is at the same time both good and loving. Our Lord contributed no philosophical explanation to the solution of this problem; He did, however, show us how to act in the face of the problem and how to conquer it. There are, consequently, certain things which can be said which partly explain it. No evil from outside can really harm one, except as one lets it do so. The evil that harms one is not what Nature or others may do to one, but that evil which one does oneself. The doctrine of free will presupposes that goodness is not a passive state, or freedom from sin, but an active state, a performance of good in face of the possibility of not doing it, which is sin or evil. Out of every evil, good can be brought and generally has been. As neither humanity nor the world has reached perfection, evil is in some way connected with the process of creation. God does not work any special favors or punishments, either to exempt from or to afflict with evil any particular person or group of persons. The goodness of one's life is no protection from physical evil, or temptation to moral evil, although it can ward off the effects of evil upon one's own character. Our Lord taught us to triumph over evil instead of letting evil triumph over us, and it is within the power of any individual who relies upon the power of God to do likewise.

THE DOCTRINE OF THE CHURCH

The Church technically consists of all who have been baptized with water in the Name of the Trinity. It is the Body of Christ made up of members of varying gifts, all acknowledging Jesus Christ as the divine Lord of their life. Not only in its members individually, but also in the

Church corporately, dwells the Holy Spirit, giving to the Church its life, and leading it and its members into all truth. The Church has been traditionally divided into the Church Militant here on earth fighting the battle against sin, the Church Expectant in the intermediate state, and the Church Triumphant in heaven. In more modern terms, the Church is one in the Lord, and her members have their fellowship with one another, both in this life and in the life to come, through their fellowship with the one Lord, their possession of the one Spirit, and their common fellowship as children of the one Father of all. This is called the Communion of Saints.

The Church exists to continue the work which Christ began upon earth, to hold up before people the revelation of God made through Jesus Christ, and to help them to attain the quality of life which God intended for them. Its corporate life is regulated and preserved through a validly appointed ministry in succession to the original apostles. Its members are strengthened and helped forward in their struggle to become Christlike through its sacraments, which are the channels of God's spiritually uplifting influence on the lives of people.

THE DOCTRINE OF THE LAST THINGS

God wills that all persons should become like His Son Jesus Christ in the moral and spiritual quality of their lives; that they should live in communion with Him, in other words, that they should live eternally. Consequently, such a life is independent of time or space. Modern Christians generally believe that there are two realms of one's existence: the first on this earth in which one dwells in a material body of flesh and blood; and the second one, which is entered through the portal of death, a spiritual realm in which one has a spiritual body fitted to the needs of such an existence and where one is set free from the limitations of time and space. This implies that the spirits of those we love who have gone before are ever present with us wherever we are.

In the next world one is set free not only from the pain of the mortal body which one possesses here, but from its needs such as food and drink; and all human distinctions based on wealth, social position, or physical prowess cease to exist. Death does not, however, end one's opportunity to progress morally and spiritually. The good and the bad are alike together in the next world as they are here, and yet there is a vast separation between them in the quality of their lives. They are living on different planes of existence. One is living in heaven, that is, with God and sharing the joys attendant upon so doing; another is living apart from Him and partaking of the misery attendant upon separation from Him. As for the judgment, that is a present thing. Our Lord is Judge in that His life is the standard by which our lives are judged, and whenever we compare our lives with His we are thereby judged. The Church, still patiently awaiting the final consummation of all things in Christ, does look forward to a time both in this world and in the next in which the power of sin will grow less and less and the influence of God's love, or grace, increasingly greater, until at last all shall attain unto the stature of Christ, which is eternal salvation.

THE CREEDS

The principal beliefs of the Church are summed up in its three great historical creeds: Apostles', Nicene, and

Athanasian. The American Church does not use the Athanasian Creed in its services, but prints it among the Historical Documents towards the end of the Prayer Book.

The Apostles' Creed

The Apostles' Creed in the Middle Ages was regarded as having been composed by the Twelve Apostles, hence its name. It certainly does contain apostolic teaching, but its formation took considerable time. It arose in the Church of Rome about 140 as a formulation of belief acknowledged by the candidate at baptism. It attained its final form in the eighth century. It is divided into twelve clauses, arranged in three sections, each having to do with One of the Persons of the Trinity.

I Believe in. Belief means an opinion upon which one is willing to act. It differs from knowledge in that one may have no actual first-hand experience of its truth or falsity. "Belief in," however, is personal and means in addition "trust in" and "surrender to in obedience."

God, the Father. God is the loving Father of all, with a personal interest in everything concerning each of His children. He is not a benevolent papa, a kindly Santa Claus, but One who loves them enough to will only what is best for them, and not just what they may happen to want.

Almighty. Although God is omnipotent, He can act only in accordance with His nature which is loving, rational, and beautiful. Therefore to our great benefit God cannot do anything evil, absurd, contradictory, or ugly.

Maker of heaven and earth. God, the Uncreated, is the Creator of all else that exists.

And in Jesus Christ. The beginning of the second section. Jesus was the personal name of our Lord. It is the
Greek form of the Hebrew name Joshua and was considered in the first century A.D. to mean "Yahweh saves,"
although its original meaning is a matter of dispute. Christ
comes from a Greek word used to translate the Hebrew
word *Messiah,* which means "Anointed One." Originally it referred to Jesus' office as God's special Representative upon earth, but soon it became used as a proper
name as well.

His only Son. God's only Son in a metaphysical sense
as a Person of the Trinity. In a different sense all Christians are sons of God by adoption in baptism.

Our Lord. Jesus is the Lord and Master of every Christian's life. In baptism we surrender ourselves to Him as
slaves and are raised by Him to be His friends and com-
panions on the way of life.

*Who was conceived by the Holy Ghost, born of the
Virgin Mary.* The doctrine of the Incarnation and virgin
birth of our Lord, which means that when God determined in the fullness of time to become Man, He Himself
started the process by which He did.

Suffered under Pontius Pilate. The historical statement
of the Passion or suffering which our Lord endured under
Pontius Pilate, the Roman procurator of Judaea from
26—36, most probably in the year 30.

Was crucified, dead, and buried. He was put to death
on a cross and actually died.

He descended into hell. Hell is a bad translation here,
as what is meant is not the place of torment, but the intermediate state. The Jews and early Christians believed
that when a person died the body lay in the grave and
the soul went to an intermediate state where it merely
existed. At the last day the soul and body were reunited,

was raised up to stand before the judgment-seat, and there sentenced according to his or her life on earth to an eternal existence of joy in heaven or of punishment in hell. It was thought that our Lord, during the period His body lay in the tomb, preached in the intermediate state to the spirits of those who had died before Him and offered them the opportunity of salvation.

The third day he rose again from the dead. In accordance with Jewish and Roman reckoning the day from which the reckoning is made is counted in as the first day. The word "again" is erroneous, and should be omitted, even if it has been part of the English Creed since before the days of the Primer. In what form our Lord rose from the dead cannot be known now with any certainty. The essential truth behind this clause is that our Lord convinced His disciples of the fact that He had overcome death and was alive.

He ascended into heaven. From a modern point of view the truth underlying the clause is that our Lord's resurrection appearances ceased and that His ministry, instead of being a local Palestinian one, became universal.

And sitteth on the right hand of God the Father almighty. The language is metaphorical and was never at any time meant to be taken literally. It is a figurative way of saying that our Lord occupies the place of honor in the Presence of God.

From thence he shall come to judge the quick and the dead. This clause refers to the belief that our Lord was going to return in glory from heaven to judge the living and the dead at the last day. Although not expecting His second coming in the near future, one does believe that He comes in judgment into each mind both in this and in the next world, and that He is both our Judge and our Standard of judgment.

I believe in the Holy Ghost. The beginning of the third section, having to do with the Holy Spirit and His work. It is quite irreverent to refer to the Holy Spirit as "It," for He is just as personal as the other two Persons of the Trinity.

The holy catholic Church. Not the Roman Catholic Church as some think. The word "catholic" comes from a Greek word meaning "universal." The clause means that one believes that our Lord founded a universal assembly of people of all races and cultures to be set apart unto righteousness to carry on His work in the world.

The communion of saints. This means the fellowship of Christians with one another through their possession of the one Spirit and their fellowship with Christ. It applies not only to this world, but also to the next. All Christians are one in Him.

The forgiveness of sins. Without which belief we should be of all most miserable, for if God always held our sins against us, no one could be saved. Before God, however, will forgive our sins, it is necessary for us to repent. Repentance involves five steps: Attrition, regret that we sinned or were caught or were punished; Contrition, sorrow that we committed the sin itself with a hatred of it; Confession, acknowledging both to God and to all that we have sinned; Satisfaction, a repairing, insofar as it is possible, of the damage caused by our sin; Amendment, which involves a change of mind and heart and will, so that what formerly was thought to be all right is now realized to be wrong, and we begin to practice the opposite virtue. When this occurs, God at once forgives us. Forgiveness is quite a different thing from the remission of the punishment for sin or the rectification of the consequences of sin, which, in this life, are under the control of human wills and natural laws and may last long after one has been forgiven by God.

The resurrection of the body, And the life everlasting. Amen. It was formerly believed that at the last day one's soul, which had been sojourning in the intermediate state, would be reunited with one's body, which would be miraculously raised from the grave to contain it. But to modern Christians these two clauses mean that we are capable of immortality; that death is not the end but a new beginning; that in the next world there is a continuity of personality with this; and that people will possess bodies belonging to the realm of this Spirit by which their personalities will be recognizable.

The Nicene Creed

At the first general council of the Church, called by the Roman Emperor Constantine in 325 at the city of Nicaea in Asia Minor, a creed was drawn up to assert the essential Deity of our Lord. At the second general council, held in 381 at Constantinople, it was further elaborated, and later still, slight additions were made. This creed in the Episcopal Church is, as a general rule, recited at the Eucharist.

I believe in one God, the Father Almighty, maker of heaven and earth, and of all of things visible and invisible. The invisible things refer historically to angelic spirits.

And in one Lord Jesus Christ, the only-begotten Son of God, begotten of his Father before all worlds, God of God, Light of Light, very God of very God, begotten, not made. This creed is in the second section extremely metaphysical. It means that the Second Person of the

Trinity is not a created being, but One eternally begotten of the Father who is the Source of the Godhead. He is true God out of true God and has always existed. He is the Light of the world, that is, the One through whom the world receives its knowledge or illumination of divine truth.

Being of one substance with the Father. It was over this clause that the great Arian controversy raged. The Son shares in the same divine essence of Deity as does the Father. As the Father is God so also is the Son God, and yet there are not two Gods but one.

By whom all things were made. The "whom" refers to the Son, who is the Agent of the Father in creation. The "by" is a bad translation and should be rendered "through." The Father was believed to have created through the intermediate agency of the Son (John 1:3,10; I Corinthians 8:6; Colossians 1:16; Hebrews 1:2).

Who for us men and for our salvation came down from heaven, and was incarnate by the Holy Ghost of the Virgin Mary, and was made man. Herein is contained the great doctrine of the Incarnation, that is, of God's taking human flesh and becoming Man to save men and women from their sins and to raise them to the moral likeness of God.

And was crucified also for us under Pontius Pilate; he suffered and was buried. The statement of Christ's Passion.

And the third day he rose again according to the Scriptures. That is, as predicted in the Jewish Old Testament. It, of course, was not written to predict the exact events of the life of Jesus Christ, although the early Christians believed that these were there foretold. They had difficulty in finding verses about the three-day resurrection. Hosea 6:2 is the one most often cited.

And ascended into heaven, and sitteth on the right hand of the Father; and he shall come again, with glory, to judge both the quick and the dead; whose kingdom shall have no end. The "whose" refers to Christ, whose Kingdom is everlasting.

And I believe in the Holy Ghost, the Lord, and Giver of Life. The Holy Spirit is not only the Source and Giver of the spiritual life, but also its Lord and Ruler. He is the Guide of the Church, continually enriching and enlarging its comprehension of the divine Truth, and hence of the divine Life.

Who proceedeth from the Father and the Son. The original creed did not have the words "and the Son." These were added later in the West. The Church in the East objected and withdrew from communion with the Western Church on this account. It is a metaphysical question about which the Church has no real knowledge. It is probably nearer the truth to say that the Spirit proceeds from the Father through the Son. However, both statements assert the same fact that the Spirit is divine in origin and is God.

Who with the Father and the Son together is worshipped and glorified. A statement that all three Persons of the Trinity are alike in honor and equally to be worshipped.

Who spake by the Prophets. Originally meaning the prophets of Judaism, it is now seen to mean that the Holy Spirit is the Inspirer of all the great prophets of the human race whether Jewish, Christian, or heathen. A prophet is one inspired to speak forth the will of God for his own generation, and does not mean here someone who predicts the future.

And I believe one holy Catholic and Apostolic Church. Unity, sanctity, catholicity, and apostolicity are the four notes or characteristics of the Church which our Lord founded.

I acknowledge one Baptism for the remission of sins. There is only one Christian baptism, that with water in the Name of the Trinity, and whoever comes to baptism repenting of former sins receives thereby the seal of God's forgiveness of those sins.

And I look for the resurrection of the dead, and the life of the world to come. Amen. In modern thought one does not look for a resurrection, but a transformed body and an immediate passage into a spiritual world in which there is continuity of memory and of personality, and where one will live forever.

These creeds, if written today, would be expressed in different language, for our whole outlook on the world has changed. Hence it is necessary to go behind their language and forms of thought to the truth which they were attempting to express, and to translate that truth into modern conceptions of the universe. The Church is a living thing, and it is essential to be loyal not to its past, but to its present in which we live.

BOOKS FOR FURTHER READING

ALLISON, C. F., *The Cruelty of Heresy.* Harrisburg, PA: Morehouse Publishing, 1994.

BAILLIE, D. M., *God Was in Christ.* New York: (Scribner) Macmillan, text edited in 1980.

BOOTY, J. E., *What Makes Us Episcopalians?* Harrisburg, PA: Morehouse Publishing, 1982.

DOCTRINE COMMISSION OF THE CHURCH OF ENGLAND, *Believing in the Church*. Harrisburg, PA: Morehouse Publishing, 1982.

LEWIS, C. S., *Mere Christianity*. New York: Macmillan, 1986.

LIVINGSTON, J. C., *Modern Christian Thought*. New York: Macmillan, 1971.

NORRIS, R. A., *Understanding the Faith of the Church*. San Francisco: HarperSF, 1984.

RICHARDSON, A., *The Westminster Dictionary of Christian Theology*. Philadelphia: Westminster/John Knox, 1983.

TAYLOR, J. V., *The Go-Between God: The Holy Spirit and the Christian Mission*. New York: Oxford University Press, 1979.

_____, ed., *We Believe in God*. Harrisburg, PA: Morehouse Publishing, 1987.

VOGEL, A. A., ed., *Theology in Anglicanism*. Harrisburg, PA: Morehouse Publishing, 1984.

WANTLAND, W. C., *Foundations of the Faith*. Harrisburg, PA: Morehouse Publishing, 1983.

WHALE, J. S., *Christian Doctrine*. New York: Cambridge University Press, 1941.

WILSON, F. E., *Faith and Practice*, rev. ed. Harrisburg, PA: Morehouse Publishing, 1992.

Chapter IX

The Church's Sacraments

"A sacrament is an outward and visible sign of an inward and spiritual grace." So runs the first part of the old catechetical definition. A sacrament is something outside of one which can be seen, symbolizing an action going on inside one's mind. Sacraments are unlimited in number, but the Church after many centuries chose seven, which, when the proper conditions are present on the part of the recipient, become the outward means of producing spiritual benefit. The seven are Holy Baptism, Holy Penance, Holy Confirmation, Holy Eucharist, Holy Matrimony, Holy Unction, and Holy Orders. Of these seven only Baptism and the Holy Eucharist are officially recognized by the Episcopal Church as Sacraments ordained by Christ as generally necessary to salvation. However, the Prayer Book provides forms for all the others of a traditionally sacramental character, without using the term "sacrament" for them, because they are not necessary in order to be saved. Many also reckon preaching among the great sacraments of the Church, others place Bible reading and hymn singing in the same category.

97

Now a sacrament consists of two parts: the outward sign and the inward grace, and the outward sign is in turn divided into two parts, the *form* and the *matter*. Some of the sacraments may be received only once, while others may be administered to a person more frequently. The various sacraments, likewise, have different requirements as to which order of the ministry may officiate at them.

BAPTISM

Baptism is the first of the sacraments which a person receives; and until one is baptized, that is, a member of the Church, one may not receive any of the others. Baptism can only be administered once. It may be administered in cases of extreme emergency by any Christian, although it is usually administered by one in priest's orders. The outward sign of baptism is, as to *matter,* water and, as to *form,* the words, *"N.,* I baptize you in the Name of the Father, and of the Son, and of the Holy Spirit." It makes no difference how the water is applied, whether by immersion or by affusion (pouring on the head), as is now ordinarily done. The inward grace is a cleansing from all sins committed previously. Water was chosen as the symbol as being the commonest of all cleansing materials. Christ is believed to have instituted baptism and its Biblical authority is found in Matthew 28:19. The sacraments, however, are not magical, and they never operate without the necessary spiritual conditions, often called a state of grace, being fulfilled upon the part of the recipient. By a state of grace is meant a state of receptivity of spiritual influence, the necessary conditions of which are faith and repentance. This comes out in the questions asked of the sponsors or of adult persons themselves before baptism. Inquiry is made as to faith in the questions whether one believes the articles of the Christian faith contained in the Apostles' Creed; and as to repentance in the questions whether one renounces evil in all its forms and purposes to follow good in accordance with God's will.

Children of a tender age, who are the persons now most ordinarily baptized, naturally seldom have any sins of their own as yet of which to repent, but by their admission into the body of persons seeking to overcome sin and to fulfill righteousness they receive forgiveness for whatever share they may have as members of the human race in the corporate and inherited sin of the race. The promises are made for them, as minors, by sureties or sponsors, who by their influence and training are expected to see that the child is brought up so as to fulfill these promises. Hence these sponsors are called godparents, that is spiritual parents. But baptism is a symbol not only of the forgiveness of sins, but also of admission into the Church. One is thereby made a member of Christ and an heir to the joyous, spiritual life promised by Christ to those who truly follow Him. It is also the time when one receives one's Christian name or names as another sign of one's new membership in Christ's Church. The bishop or priest also places a hand on the candidate's head and marks the forehead with the sign of the cross (using Chrism, which is oil consecrated by a bishop, if desired) and says: "*N.*, you are sealed by the Holy Spirit in Baptism and marked Christ's own for ever" (*cf.* II Corinthians 1:22; Ephesians 1:13, 4:30). From now on the baptized person's life should be under the guidance of the Holy Spirit, in the joy of His inward Presence, and marked by the humility of one who has been signed with the cross.

PENANCE

Penance is the sacrament symbolizing the forgiveness of sins committed after baptism. It may be administered by anyone in priest's orders as often as there is need. Its Biblical warrant is found in John 20:22,23. The outward sign consists of the form "I absolve you from all your sins: In the Name of the Father, and of the Son, and of the Holy Spirit. Amen." Absolution does not effect the forgiveness of sins; it is an outward sign to the penitent heart of God's forgiveness, which is dependent solely on one's repentance. Confession is made privately to God in the presence of His priest for both God and humanity are outraged by sin. It is made in the presence of a priest to deepen one's humility, to judge the sincerity of one's repentance, and to give counsel which will be helpful in overcoming sin in the future.

The absolution pronounced by the priest after the general confessions in Morning and Evening Prayer and the Eucharist is a general absolution in a precatory form and applicable, as all absolutions, only to those who are sincerely penitent and faithfully believe God's holy promises of forgiveness.

CONFIRMATION

Confirmation is the sacrament of the impartation of spiritual strength to lead the Christian life. It is generally administered at that time of life when one ceases to be a child spiritually and becomes a spiritual adult. It is the ordination of the laity by the laying-on-of-hands to their own sacred ministry of full service and responsibility in God's Church. Confirmation can only be administered once and, in the Anglican Communion, only by a bishop as the successor of the apostles. Its Biblical warrant is found in Acts 8:14-17, 19:1-7; Hebrews 6:2. The outward sign consists, as to *matter,* of the laying on of the bishop's hands upon the head of the person confirmed, and, as to *form,* the prayer said as he does it. Confirmation is not something magical to make a person good overnight, nor is it what makes one an Episcopalian; but it is the outward assurance of God's gift of His own spiritual strength and influence to vanquish evil and to carry out His will. This spiritual influence may be neglected, and in time it will grow weak, or it may be cultivated and thereby increased; but Confirmation is the outward symbol to all that their bodies are the temples of the Holy Ghost and that He is capable if they will but follow, of leading them into all truth and righteousness and peace.

EUCHARIST

The Holy Eucharist is the sacrament in which the soul is nourished with spiritual food; through it one receives the sustenance of one's spiritual life. The Eucharist may be celebrated by anyone in priest's orders as often as the occasion may arise, although custom limits this, except in cases of necessity, to once during each ecclesiastical day, measured from midnight to midnight. The outward sign, as to *matter,* is bread and wine, the commonest forms of food and drink in the Orient of Christ's time; and, as to *form,* the words with which our Lord Himself instituted the Sacrament: "This is My Body," "This is My Blood." Accounts of the institution of the Holy Eucharist are found in Matthew 26:26-28; Mark 14:22-25;

Luke 22:19, 20; I Corinthians 11:23-26. A person not in priest's orders should make his Communion only once within the period from midnight to midnight, although one may attend as many celebrations as one wishes.

There are many aspects of the Eucharist, some of which are indicated by the various names it has been called in the course of time. The common Anglican name "Holy Communion" suggests the fact that it is in and through this sacrament that one enters into that communion and fellowship with God wherein one unites one's purposes with His and surrenders one's will to Him, and labors together with Him in joyous companionship for the establishment of His rule in the world. It also symbolizes the communion of Christians with one another through their communion with the Lord.

The name "Holy Sacrifice" brings to mind the great central fact that this sacrament is a commemoration and memorial of Christ's sacrifice upon the cross, of Love giving Himself in self-sacrifice for those whom He loved. It is a reminder that insofar as one through love sacrifices oneself for others, one shares in the divine life.

The name "Holy Eucharist," which is a Greek word for thanksgiving, emphasizes the fact that this sacrament is one way of publicly expressing our gratitude to God for the innumerable benefits which have come to us from the life, death, and resurrection of Christ. In thankfulness to Him for these, the Christian in this sacrament seeks the power to make his or her life more nearly like His.

The name "The Lord's Supper" brings out the fact that it is through this means that the Lord nourishes our souls, by our offering of them to God for His service, and receiving them back freshened and strengthened through contact with His Presence. It also commemorates the Last Supper which our Lord had with His apostles.

The name "the Divine Liturgy" stresses that when we worship God, it is a work or service which we do for Him.

In the Roman Church, it is called "the Mass," which has no special meaning and apparently is derived from the closing words of the service in Latin, *"Ite, missa est."*

Devout Christians truly believe in the Real Presence of our Lord in the Sacrament which He instituted, but also believe that He is only perceived by faith. Various theologians have attempted to define more closely the exact manner of His Presence, such as the Romans by transubstantiation and the Lutherans by consubstantiation; many limiting it to the consecrated Bread and Wine. The important thing is not how our Lord is present in the Sacrament, but that through the Sacrament His Presence becomes real in the life of the person receiving it.

One should come to the Holy Communion as often as one has need, but it will be found that if one's perception of one's need is not increasing, one's spiritual life is dwindling and not growing. Persons recently confirmed would do well, as a general rule, to come at least once a month their first year thereafter, and then to increase the number of times gradually until they make their Communion at least once a week.

Each time that one comes to the Holy Communion one should come with a definite intention, around which one's prayers and aspirations should center, knowing precisely for what one is going to give thanks and pray and what one is going to confess. One has too large a task to accomplish to dissipate one's spiritual desires and energies on a vague wish to be better or a confused petition for strength or help; what one needs is guidance and support for the immediate task. Consequently, one may come to the Eucharist with a desire to be more loving and less jealous, and with a particular person or persons in mind towards whom, with God's help, one is going to make a definite act of goodwill. Or one may come with the intention of thanking God for some particular blessing or blessings to oneself or others; or with a particular intercession in mind for those in this life, the next, or for some cause or organization in which one is interested; at the same time freely offering oneself as an instrument for the accomplishment of the petition. In this way, by definitely centering the mind on a particular object and entering into fellowship with God with this in mind, spiritual energy is concentrated on a particular task with an effectiveness which is never present when one comes vaguely to the Sacrament without such intention or preparation.

It is, furthermore, expected that every person before receiving the Sacrament will have carefully examined his or her life in the light of the divine life and repented fully of all that is not in conformity therewith; and, as the General Confession is said, have his or her own particular sins in mind. Custom forbids receiving the Sacrament if one is not in church in time to say the Confession.

The necessary conditions of receiving the Holy Communion are set forth in the invitation in the Prayer Book: "Ye who do truly and earnestly repent you of your sins, and are in love and charity with your neighbors, and intend to lead a new life, following the commandments of God, and walking from henceforth in His holy ways: Draw near with faith, and make your humble confession to Almighty God, devoutly kneeling." They are the same two requirements as for the reception of the other sacraments: faith and repentance. The positive side of repentance is here fully brought out in the requirement that one must wish all well and that each Communion should be a new dedication to God and His will, the renewal of one's spiritual life.

MATRIMONY

One does not need to come to the Church to be married, and those who do should not only be members of the Church, but have every intention of living their married life in accordance with God's will. There is a difference between mere marriage and Holy Matrimony. The outward sign of matrimony is a contract between a man and a woman to live together as husband and wife, of which the giving and receiving of a ring and the joining of hands are the symbol. The inner meaning is the union of the two lives into one. Genesis 2:24 and Mark 10:7–9 are generally cited as the Biblical references to the institution of this sacrament. The law specifies who may perform marriages, but only one in priest's orders may bless a marriage, and that is really all that the Church does. After vows duly given and the contract made, they begin their married life by praying the Lord's Prayer. Then the Church prays that the two lives may become spiritually one, that each may live for the other, and that they together may work as one for the accomplishment of God's purposes in the world. Consequently, the Church should not be asked, and should refuse to bless any marriage in which it does not find such an intention present.

UNCTION

Unction is the sacrament whereby the sick are anointed with oil for spiritual and bodily healing. It may be administered as often as need requires, but only by one in priest's orders. The warrant for it is found in James 5:14. Its outward sign as to *matter* is oil, and to *form*, "*N.*, I anoint you with oil, in the Name of the Father, and of the Son, and of the Holy Spirit. Amen."

Oil was chosen as the symbol because it has from ancient times been a healing remedy. The sacrament proclaims God's power to heal both the body and the soul, but there is nothing magical about it. When it is administered to sensible people who are penitent and full of faith, it can be of help in predisposing their minds to health and hope, and in centering their trust on God.

ORDERS

Holy Orders is the sacrament wherein the authority to act as ministers in Christ's Church is conferred, and the spiritual strength necessary to fulfil the task is imparted. It can only be conferred once for each of the three orders of bishops, priests, and deacons, for it conveys a *character indelebilis* which can never be taken away, although one may be deposed, that is, deprived of the right to exercise the office. Biblical references to ordination are found in Matthew 28:18–20; John 20:21–23; Acts 6:5,6, 13:2,3; I Timothy 3:1–10; Titus 1:5–9. Ordination in Anglican, Greek, and Roman communions can only be administered by a bishop, although priests assist in the laying on of hands at ordination to the priesthood. At the consecration of a new bishop the participation of at least three bishops in apostolic succession is required. The outward sign, as to *matter,* is the laying on of the bishop's hands upon the head of the person to be ordained, and the *form* is a formula for each order specifying the office and its purpose. The inner grace is God's sustaining strength and guidance for those who have been given authority to minister in His Name. The ministry is a sacrament, in that it is a channel through which God's revelation and strength and forgiveness and blessing are brought to His children.

A deacon may read Morning and Evening Prayer, the Litany, Ante-Communion, and the Burial Service; preach (when licensed thereto by the bishop); baptize (in the absence of a priest); and assist at the Holy Eucharist and the other sacraments. A priest may, in addition, absolve penitent persons from sins; bless in the Name of the Lord; and consecrate the bread and the wine in the Holy Communion to be the Body and Blood of Christ. These three powers are sometimes referred to as the priestly ABC. In addition to these, a bishop has power to confirm people with the Holy Spirit; and to ordain men and women to the ministry.

Through these seven sacraments, as through many other channels, the life of God is constantly being infused into the life of all, vitalizing it into a new life, the life eternal.

BOOKS FOR FURTHER READING

EASTMAN, A. T., *The Baptizing Community, Christian Initiation and the Local Congregation.* Harrisburg, PA: Morehouse Publishing, 1991.
GULICK, A., *This Bread, This Cup: An Introduction to the Eucharist.* Harrisburg, PA: Morehouse Publishing, 1992.
HYDE, C., *To Declare God's Forgiveness, Toward a Pastoral Theology of Reconciliation.* Harrisburg, PA: Morehouse Publishing, 1984.

WEBBER, C. L. and M., *Planning Your Marriage Service.* Harrisburg, PA: Morehouse Publishing, 1992.

WEBBER, C. L., *Re-Inventing Marriage.* Harrisburg, PA: Morehouse Publishing, 1994.

Chapter X

The Church's Requirements

The Church is not the ministry nor do the church buildings belong to the ministers. The Church is the whole body of those who have been made members of Christ through Baptism, and each member is responsible for its welfare and shares in its privileges. One should therefore memorize the question and answer from the 1928 Prayer Book Second Office of Instruction, and perform it. *"Question.* What is your bounden duty as a member of the Church? *Answer.* My bounden duty is to follow Christ, to worship God every Sunday in his Church; and to work and pray and give for the spread of his kingdom."

The first and great obligation of every Christian, then, is to be a faithful follower of Christ and a good Church member who will support the Church — support it by prayers, by regular attendance at its services of worship, by participation in its activities, by commendation of it to others, and by giving to it in accordance with his or her means.

A Christian should remember every day in prayer not only the Church at large with all its work, but his or her own particular parish with all its needs, its clergy, and its other members, and should each night seriously consider whether he or she is doing his or her own part in its support, and pray to be a better member.

The question should never arise on Sunday as to whether one should go to church or not; that should be taken for granted. For members of the Episcopal Church are bound by Canon II.1, which reads: "All persons within this Church shall celebrate and keep the Lord's Day, commonly called Sunday, by regular participation in the public worship of the Church, by hearing the Word of God read and taught, and by other acts of devotion and works of charity, using all godly and sober conversation." The question may arise occasionally as to whether one should stay away on account of illness or some other grave cause, but never on account of the visit of friends or relations. If they will not go to church, one's first duty is to God and not to them. One should also see how many of the weekday services one is able to attend, and support them as well. No matter how dull the sermon, or how mechanically or badly read the service, one can always speak to God and let Him speak to one's heart; and furthermore, there is always the lesson of patience to be learned, until one takes loving steps to correct what is at fault.

Every man, woman, and child, insofar as they are able, should be a member of, and whole-heartedly support the church societies and activities for which they are fitted, in order that the friendly life of service of the parish may be increased. Never wait to be asked to join a church organization. Make your desire to serve known to the rector, and let him or her place you where you are most needed.

Nowhere does there seem to be more gossip and back-biting and criticism, sometimes, than in church work.

And this is a positive hindrance to the furtherance of its purpose of loving service. A Church member should not only refrain from such talk, but do all in his or her power to commend their own parish and church to all. A good rule might well be: "To say nothing of the Church except that which is good."

It is amazing how few who call themselves Christians actively support the Church financially. They think that an occasional quarter or dollar bill placed in the plate when they happen to be present discharges their financial obligation. Or else they feel that the Church is only to be supported out of their surplus; and when their financial situation changes for the worse, it is perfectly proper to economize by ceasing to give to the Church altogether. Others think that because one member of the family contributes it is not necessary for the other members to do so. Even where the money eventually all comes from one member of the family, each of the others should be given an allowance, for this purpose if for no other, in order that he may definitely feel himself a contributor. This applies to boys and girls who have been confirmed just as much as to older people. In very few, if any, cases would it be impossible for those who really wanted to do so to give a dime a week to the support of the Church, and they could contribute their time and services in other ways which would save the Church money and thus be an actual financial contribution as well. The Church expects a person to regard all his or her wealth as held in trust for God and to apportion his or her income for the good of others, including the Church, as God may direct. The 1982 General Convention called upon all Episcopalians to accept "the biblical tithe as the minimum standard of Christian giving."

A Church member should also take an intelligent interest in parochial affairs and attend the annual Parish Meeting. One should keep oneself posted on what the Church is doing. The most helpful way of accomplishing this is to subscribe to the monthly magazine issued under the auspices of General Convention, *The Episcopalian;* or one of the national Church papers, *The Living Church, The Witness,* or *The Anglican Digest.*

A Church member should also read the Bible regularly and be intelligently acquainted with the history, doctrine, and customs of the Church. Religious education is not meant to be confined to the period of attendance in the church school, but should be co-extensive with a person's life from the cradle to the grave. One should seek to interest others in the Church and should invite them to come to church. And one should so conduct oneself at all times that people may know that he or she is a Christian, and that God and His Church may thus be praised.

A Church member moving from one parish to another should request a letter of transfer from the former parish to the new one. Only in this way can the records and statistics of the Church be kept anywhere nearly accurate. It also helps to establish standing in the new parish at once. All that is needed to do is to write the former rector requesting a letter of transfer and stating the name of the new parish. Some people hesitate to do this for sentimental reasons; others to escape financial responsibility in the new parish; but every Church member who places the well-being of the Church first will do so at once.

Parents are charged with the responsibility of bringing their children up as members of God's family, which means, first of all, making them such in Baptism. From the parents' point of view Baptism is a dedication on their part of their child to God, to grow up in His love, and to go forth to do His work in the world. Secondly, they are responsible for creating a family life in accordance with God's will, a home where a child will feel the Presence and influence of God. Thirdly, they are charged with seeing that their children are instructed in the Christian religion and have ample opportunity for participating in its worship and work at home and school and church. Parents can only effectively discharge these obligations by example, rather than precept; that is, by living the Christian life themselves.

Godparents should be baptized, and preferably confirmed members of the Episcopal Church, with an affection not only for the parents and child, but also for God and His Church. They should be people to whose lives a child can look for inspiration and guidance as to how to live more like Christ; and consequently, they should be people with whom the child may reasonably be expected to come frequently in contact. It is their duty, as well as that of the parents, to see that the child is instructed in the Christian religion; learns the Creed, the Lord's Prayer, and the Ten Commandments; and is actively striving to fulfil the promises they made in his or her name, by keeping from evil, and growing in love for God and humanity, and in all that is beautiful, true, and good. Traditionally the godparents are three in number: two of the same sex as the child, and one of the opposite.

As a member of the Church a person is entitled free to its spiritual ministrations of all kinds; and by this is meant the use of the church buildings and the services of the clergy. Those, however, who want special music or decorations for a service must necessarily pay the cost involved. The clergy consider it a privilege to be able to minister in any way to those who are in trouble or in sorrow, to those weighed down with sin or care, to the sick and to the dying, and to those whose lives are filled with joy. In a large parish, and often even in a small one, it is impossible for the clergy always to know when they are needed, and they look to the persons themselves and to their friends to inform them when they can be of service. Clergy are in duty bound to baptize a dying person at any time when called upon, and likewise to hear a confession of sin when a person's conscience is greatly troubled. They will gladly arrange to have a private celebration of the Eucharist at home or at a hospital for anyone who is ill or prevented by infirmity from attending church, and they expect as a matter of course to bring their Christmas and Easter Communions to those unable to be in church. It is a Church member's privilege to consult the pastor at any time in regard to spiritual and moral questions. Here, as always, people will realize that, due to the manifold demands on a modern minister's time, it is well to make an appointment in advance, in order that the convenience of both may best be suited.

For more than a thousand years many people have found it spiritually helpful to receive the Holy Eucharist fasting, that is neither eating nor drinking from the midnight preceding until they have communicated. Since afternoon and evening Eucharist services have become fairly widespread, this is no longer practical. The best custom seems to be to abstain from solid food and alcoholic drink for three hours before communicating in the afternoon and evening, and from all liquids for one hour previously. The Episcopal Church has no binding requirement in this matter.

Before a Baptism, the parents should arrange a time for the minister to give them and the godparents the required instruction in the significance of Holy Baptism and their responsibility in the Christian training of the child. In regard to marriages and burials, the clergy should always be consulted first, rather than the sexton or undertaker, as to the day and time of the service. The clergy are required by canon law, except for weighty reasons when one of the parties is known, to have at least thirty days' notice before performing a marriage service, and to see that the bride and groom are instructed as to the nature, meaning, and purpose of Holy Matrimony. Unless there are good reasons to the contrary, all baptisms, marriages, and burials should be held in the church.

The Christian ideal of marriage is a lifelong union of a man and a woman, each living for the other, and both for the children whom they may produce, in a home of happiness and peace. Just as the death of one of the partners legally ends the marriage, so also the death of the marriage itself may be ended legally by annulment or divorce. In such unfortunate cases, if either or both of the parties wish to remarry while the other is alive, they must obtain the consent of the diocesan bishop through their minister before they can be married again in an Episcopal church. But it is within the discretion of any minister to decline to the solemnize any marriage.

If there is anything about the Church or its ways or teaching that one does not understand, one should consult the pastor, who will be sympathetic with the ignorance and proud of the interest and only too glad to help in any way that he or she can. Good pastors refuse to belittle parishioners by assuming that they will do anything less than their full duty as members of Christ's Church.

FOR FURTHER READING

BOOTY, J. E., *The Servant Church*. Harrisburg, PA: Morehouse Publishing, 1982.

FARNHAM, S., *et. al.*, *Listening Hearts: Discerning Call in Community*. Harrisburg, PA: Morehouse Publishing, 1991.

Constitution and Canons for the Government of the Protestant Episcopal Church in the United States of America, (revised every three years).

The Anglican Digest. Published quarterly by SPEAK, 100 Skyline Drive, Eureka Springs, Arkansas 72632-9705.

Episcopal Life. Published monthly, 815 Second Ave., New York, New York 10017.

The Living Church. Published weekly by The Living Church Foundation, P.O. Box 92936, Milwaukee, Wisconsin 53202-0936.

The Witness. Published monthly by The Episcopal Church Publishing Company, 1249 Washington Blvd., Suite 3115, Detroit, Michigan 48226.

Appendices

Appendix A

Preparation for Confirmation

There is no "correct" age for Confirmation. The proper time varies with each individual. Children should have reached years of discretion, that is, spiritual maturity. They should be stable and dependable, with a comprehension of the fundamental difference between what is right and what is wrong, and an earnest desire to follow the right. In addition, they should have some background and acquaintance with the Church and its teaching. Normally this occurs with most children about the age of puberty. But it is always possible to confirm children who have been brought up in religious homes where the parents regularly attend and support the Church earlier than those from homes where they would have to stand alone in maintaining their religious ideals. It must also be remembered that the age when the parents or other children in the family were confirmed has little to do with the case of the particular child being considered. Adults should be confirmed whenever they are sufficiently acquainted with the ways and teachings of the Episcopal Church to be convinced that they wish to make it their

119

permanent spiritual home; and, in addition, feel a sense of rededication to God and a consequent desire for the strengthening aid of His Holy Spirit.

There are two preparations to be made before being confirmed, one of the heart and the other of the mind; although the preparation is really not so much for Confirmation, as for the whole period of one's life afterwards. Furthermore, it is not a question of being prepared for Confirmation, but rather of preparing oneself. The preparation of the mind is secured through the attendance at a Confirmation class, or through private interviews with clergy, and by the reading of Confirmation manuals and other books about the Church and its ways and teaching. In order to be an intelligent, helpful, loyal Church member, one must have some knowledge of these things, a distinct understanding of what is expected of one as a member, and a feeling of familiarity with the doctrine and worship which puts one at ease during the service and allows one's thoughts to center upon God. For this reason one should first of all read through the entire Prayer Book, note its contents, and study the sections entitled "An Outline of the Faith" and "Historical Documents of the Church."

The preparation of the heart is harder and must be made largely alone, although the clergy will always be glad to help with what counsel they can. As soon as one knows when the bishop is coming for Confirmation, and has decided after careful thought and consultation with one's rector and family to be confirmed at that time, one should make an act of surrender to God. It should be in intention an act of complete surrender of one's whole life, although in practice such an act of complete surrender comes rather at the end than at the beginning of the adult Christian life. One does not have to feel good or righteous or holy to be confirmed. If one does, it is probably due to pride and the person is not ready for Confirmation. What one must feel is the desire to be better each day, and the determination to make one's life increasingly like that of Christ.

Secondly, one should determine that one's Confirmation preparation shall take precedence over everything else, and accordingly set apart the time necessary for the Confirmation classes and for one's outside study and Bible reading. If one has not already established the habit of saying one's prayers daily both in the morning and in the evening, one should begin to do so.

The next step is to make a thorough examination of one's past and present life, and one's hopes and aspirations for the future, and to see how nearly they conform to the standards of Christ. Having done so, one should confess one's sins to God, make proper satisfaction for them insofar as that is possible, and then actively take measures to grow in the opposite virtues. An aid to such self-examination will be found in Appendix B.

Fourthly, one should remember in one's prayers morning and night the Church, the bishop who is to confirm, the minister preparing one for Confirmation, the other members of the Confirmation class, and one's own particular needs, including a petition that one may uphold one's full responsibility as a member of the Church.

The night before Confirmation one should again examine one's life and confess one's sins to God; review the solemn promises of renunciation, faith, and obedience which one is to assume for oneself; and, determining to live in communion with God, open one's heart to Him with complete trust that it may be filled with His Holy Spirit, and that thus, day by day, one may grow more like Christ.

Some people are worried by the question of how they should be dressed for Confirmation. There are two simple rules: First of all, be neatly and soberly dressed; and secondly, insofar as it is financially possible, follow the parish custom. In many parishes it is customary for the women and girls to be dressed entirely in white and to wear white veils, and for the boys and men to wear dark suits, white shirts, ties, dark socks, and polished dark shoes; in others for both the men and women merely to be quietly dressed, and for the women, if wearing hats, to remove them before coming forward to be presented to the bishop.

A Confirmation class may consist of those who have been baptized in the Episcopal or some other Church and wish to be confirmed; those who have already been confirmed by a bishop in the apostolic succession not in communion with the Episcopal Church, such as the Roman Catholic, and wish to be received; and those who have been baptized and confirmed at the same time as infants and wish to reaffirm their baptismal covenant themselves and assume their adult role in the Church. Generally the class will sit together as a group in the front pews.

Since the new Prayer Book, Confirmation may take place in three different ways. There may be a service, such as the primitive Church held during the Easter Vigil, conducted by a bishop, consisting of Baptism, Confirmation, and Holy Eucharist, when all three sacraments are administered immediately following each other. Customarily, however, Confirmation is administered within the Holy Eucharist, when a person is confirmed and receives the Communion at the same time. The service may also be held by itself; but in all three cases it begins with that part of the Eucharist known as "The Word of

God," omitting the penitential part, and continues through the sermon.

During a hymn after the sermon the candidates come forward from their pews according to their grouping, and stand before the bishop, seated in his chair on the gospel side, and are presented by the rector or other clergy. All are now questioned as to their renunciation of evil, commitment to Christ, and acceptance of the Baptismal Covenant. Its first three questions have to do with the three sections of the Apostles' Creed, after which the candidates repeat that part of the Creed in a modern translation. Five other questions in regard to their willingness to lead the Christian life follow, and the bishop then prays over them. Those baptized as infants have now taken the responsibility for their spiritual welfare from their godparents and assumed it themselves. All of these promises have been summed up as: to renounce what is evil, to believe what is true, and to do what is good. They are the most solemn promises of one's life, and should only be taken after much prayer and the serious consideration of all that is involved in so doing.

Then the Confirmation candidates kneel at the altar rail, or else come individually and kneel before the bishop seated in a chair before the altar. He lays his hands upon them individually and confirms them with a prayer, in which he uses the person's baptismal name. Those being received are welcomed with his right hand as he prays over them. He may make the sign of the cross over those reaffirming their baptismal vows as he prays for them. After a final prayer the peace is exchanged. The service either continues with the Eucharist, or ends with the Lord's Prayer and other devotions. During a hymn the class returns to its pews. There is always an offering, which is customarily given to the bishop's discretionary fund. Each member of the class should be prepared to contribute a personal thank-offering. After the service it is usual for the class to greet the bishop and receive their certificates. When a confirmed or received person makes Communion at this time or later, he or she becomes officially a communicant of the Episcopal Church; although all along since Baptism he or she has been a member of Christ's Church.

BOOKS FOR FURTHER READING

ATWATER, G. P., *The Episcopal Church: Its Message for Today.* Harrisburg, PA: Morehouse Publishing, 1978.

FERGUSON, F. C., *A Pilgrimage in Faith.* Harrisburg, PA: Morehouse Publishing, 1979.

KRUMM, J. M., *Why Choose the Episcopal Church?* Cincinnati: Forward Movement, 1974.

Appendix B

An Aid to Self-Examination

Have I loved God with all my
    heart?
    soul?
    mind?

Have I prayed to Him morning and night?

Have I supported His Church and His worship with
    my presence?
    my participation in its activities?
    my money?

Have I been reverent at all times?

Have I sought to know His will?
    and to do it?

Have I sought to make God known to others?

Have I loved my neighbor as myself?

Have I unselfishly placed the welfare of others above
    my own?

Have I always wished and done all persons well?

Have I worked and prayed for a more equitable social
  order?

Have I, in the meantime, done my part to support the
  charities and social agencies seeking to alleviate
  present suffering?

Have I prayed and worked for international peace?

Have I done my part to live at peace with all people?

Have I been chaste and pure in
  mind?
  speech?
  body?

Have I been humble and modest in bearing?
  speech?
  dress?

Have I been honest in all my dealings with
  persons?
  companies?
  governments?

Have I been merciful, kind, and tolerant in
  thought?
  word?
  deed?

Have I held myself in self-control?
  particularly in regard to my tongue?

Have I been courageous and brave?

Have I been patient under affliction?

Have I been joyous and the bringer of cheer to heavy-
  laden hearts?

Have I been loyal to all to whom my loyalty is due?

Appendix C

Prayers

In Preparation for Confirmation

O God, who through the teaching of thy Son Jesus Christ didst prepare the disciples for the coming of the Comforter: Make ready, I beseech thee, the hearts and minds of us who, at this time, are seeking to be strengthened by the gift of the Holy Spirit through the laying on of hands; that, drawing near with penitent and faithful hearts, we may evermore be filled with the power of his divine indwelling; through the same Jesus Christ our Lord. Amen.

O Lord God, Giver of heavenly increase, who by the might of thy Spirit dost confirm the first efforts of my soul: Encourage in me every good intent, and carry me from strength to strength. Cleanse my conscience, and stir my will gladly to serve thee, the living God. Leave no room in me for spiritual wickedness, no lurking-place for secret sins; but so establish and sanctify me by the power of thy holy Word, that, evermore taking heed unto the thing which is right, and speaking and doing the truth, I may find godliness my gain, both in the life which now is, and in that which is to come; through Jesus Christ my Lord. Amen.

O Lord and heavenly Father, who art calling us at this time to seek thy grace in Confirmation and to dedicate our lives to thy service: Prepare us, we pray thee, for this solemn ordinance, and make us faithful members of thy Church. Open our hearts to receive all that thou art waiting to bestow upon us. Teach us more of thy truth, more of thy love, more of thyself. And grant that, in lives made strong by thy Holy Spirit, we may serve thee gladly and bravely all our days; for the sake of Jesus Christ our Lord. Amen.

Grant, Almighty God, that we, who have been redeemed from the old life of sin by our baptism into the death and resurrection of thy Son Jesus Christ, may be renewed in thy Holy Spirit, and grow in righteousness and true holiness; through the same Jesus Christ our Lord, who liveth and reigneth with thee and thy same Spirit, one God, now and forever. Amen.

Lord God of hosts, my Captain and my King: Accept, I pray thee, us that are about to offer thee the service of our lives. Make our wills strong, our courage steadfast, and our faith firm; that, having been signed in baptism with the cross, and now of our own will enlisting in that service, we may not be ashamed to confess the faith of Christ crucified, but manfully fight under his banner against sin, the world, and the devil, and continue Christ's faithful soldiers and servants unto our life's end. Amen.

O Lord God, who hast sent thy Holy Spirit into the world to strengthen me and to lead me into all truth: I pray thee that I, believing in thy promises and trusting in thy love, may be so prepared by thee to receive the grace of Confirmation, that I may come with a faithful and penitent heart unto that holy mystery, and may obtain the fullness of those gifts which thou dost promise, so that I may have strength to resist all sin, and grace to persevere unto the end; through Jesus Christ my Lord. Amen.

Strengthen, O Lord, I pray thee, by thy Holy Spirit, those who are now preparing to seek thy help in Confirmation; and grant that all of us who wear the Cross upon our foreheads, may bear it also in our hearts; so that, boldly confessing thee before all, we may be found worthy to be numbered among thy saints; through Jesus Christ our Lord. Amen.

In Preparation for the Holy Communion

O Lord, my Master, prepare me to receive thee in the Holy Communion; then come in all thy might. Let thy strength make me strong, thy purity make me pure, thy gentleness make me kind; that, as thy fellow worker, I may help to make this world a better place according to thy will; who art God for ever and ever. Amen.

Grant me, O Lord, the help of thy grace, that at this holy Sacrament I may bring all my thoughts and desires into subjection to thy holy will, and may offer my soul and body a living sacrifice unto thee, in union with the perfect sacrifice of thy Son, my Savior Jesus Christ. Amen.

O Almighty God, whose blessed Son did institute and ordain holy mysteries as pledges of his love, and for a continual remembrance of his death: Mercifully grant that I, and all who shall come to thy Holy Table, may be filled with a deep sense of the exceeding holiness of this blessed mystery; and that, drawing near with true, penitent hearts and lively faith, in love and charity with all, we may worthily receive that holy Sacrament, and obtain the fullness of thy grace, to our present comfort and our everlasting salvation; through the same Jesus Christ our Lord. Amen.

O God, who dost govern the thoughts of all: Bring to my mind the upper room where the Lord Jesus broke bread with his disciples the night before he was crucified. Grant that, being of that company, I may look into the face of him who gave himself for the world. While I eat of his bread and drink of his cup, fill my life with his life; and send me forth to think his thoughts, to say his words, to do his deeds. And so, O blessed Father, grant that the light of his face may shine in my face, that all may take note that I have been with Jesus; who liveth and reigneth with thee and the Holy Spirit, the God of everlasting love. Amen.

On Entering Church

Our heavenly Father, strengthen the work of this Church for the good of thy children; guide and support those who minister here in thy service; open the hearts of those who worship here to receive thy wisdom and to do thy will; and help me reverently and attentively to worship thee, and day by day to grow more like thy Son, Jesus Christ our Lord. Amen.

On Leaving Church

O Lord, I thank thee for this time of worship, and pray that it may bring me and all here into closer fellowship with thee and with one another, that so we may go forth strengthened to serve thee more faithfully all our days; through Jesus Christ our Savior. Amen.

Graces

O Lord, bless this food to our nourishment, that we may be strengthened for thy service; through Jesus Christ our Savior. Amen.

O Lord, from whom all good things do come: We pray thee to bless this food. Give us grateful hearts, and make us mindful of the needs of others; for Christ's sake we ask it. Amen.

For these and all his mercies, God's holy Name be praised; through Christ our Lord. Amen.

Appendix D

A Partial List of Christian Religious Classics

The Apostolic Fathers.
The Confessions of St. Augustine.
The Little Flowers of St. Francis of Assisi.
The Divine Comedy, by Dante Alighieri.
The Imitation of Christ, by Thomas á Kempis.
The Revelations of Mother Juliana of Norwich.
Theologia Germanica.
The Spiritual Exercises of St. Ignatius Loyola.
Spiritual Letters of St. Francis de Sales.
Private Prayers of Lancelot Andrewes.
Paradise Lost, by John Milton.
Holy Living and Holy Dying, by Jeremy Taylor.
The Pilgrim's Progress, by John Bunyan.
The Practice of the Presence of God, by Brother Lawrence.
A Serious Call to a Devout and Holy Life, by William Law.
The Christian Year, by John Keble.